VISIONS OF THE CAILLEACH

"Determined now her tomb to build,
Her ample skirt with stones she filled,
And dropped a heap on Carron-more;
Then stepped one thousand yards to Loar,
And dropped another goodly heap;
And then with one prodigious leap,
Gained carrion-beg; and on its height
Displayed the wonders of her might."

Jonathan Swift (1667 – 1745)

VISIONS

OF THE

CAILLEACH

*Exploring the Myths, Folklore and Legends of
the pre-eminent Celtic Hag Goddess*

Sorita d'Este & David Rankine

Published by Avalonia

BM Avalonia
London
WC1N 3XX
England, UK

www.avaloniabooks.co.uk

VISIONS OF THE CAILLEACH

ISBN (10) 1-905297-24-6
ISBN (13) 978-1-905297-24-5

First Edition, 25 March 2009
Design by Satori

Cover Art *"Old Woman in the Hedge"* © Marc Potts

Old Woman in the Hedge, **by Marc Potts**

For more information about this British artist, visit his website:

www.marcpotts.com

This book is dedicated to our grandmothers.

CONTENTS

INTRODUCTION

The Cailleach is one of the most intriguing and significant figures in British folklore. Some tales portray her as a benevolent and primal giantess from the dawn of time who shaped the land and controlled the forces of nature, others as the harsh spirit of winter. Occasionally there are hints that she may represent the survival of an early sovereignty bestowing earth goddess, or an ancient nature-based priestess cult. In the last twelve hundred years the Christian overlay has both demonised and canonised her.

Although the stories of the Cailleach are essentially British, her origins are not. Exploring the earliest literary references to the Cailleach takes us to the classics of ancient Greece and Rome. References in writings by Herodotus, Strabo and Pliny suggest her worship as a Celtic tutelary goddess on the Iberian peninsula of Spain two and a half thousand years ago.

Moving beyond literature and focusing on the similarities in motifs, such as her giant size and stone-carrying, leads us to Neolithic Malta. There are distinct similarities between the Cailleach and the Maltese giantess Sansuna, credited by legend with building the Ggantija temples on the island of Gozo. These impressive buildings are the oldest religious structures in the world, predating monuments like the Pyramids and Stonehenge.

From such ancient Mediterranean origins, the Cailleach migrated with the Celts from Spain to Ireland, and on to Scotland and the Isle of Man. It is possible that her worship and stories also spread into the rest of Britain, hinted at in local folklore and place names. Thus we find possible echoes of her presence in England, Wales, and Jersey. The continental connection is also reinforced in shared motifs found in Brittany (France) and Scandinavia.

More than any other figure in Celtic or British myth, the Cailleach represents the cumulative power of time. Her great age is a common theme in many of the tales about her, and as a result she has almost always been seen as a hag or crone (a meaning of her name). Her earth-shaping ability, through accidental placement of great stones expresses a mythic explanation for processes which take millions of years. The deliberate placement of stones is frequently tied in with Neolithic burial chambers, hinting at the survival of a cult from the distant past.

The Cailleach also has strong associations with both the weather and water, being viewed as the goddess of the harsh winter months. In this role she has been linked in literature and legend to the Celtic maiden goddess Bride, sometimes as polar opposite and at other times as being dual manifestations of the same goddess. The extent of her power was made clear when she exercised her control over the forces of nature, which made her a significant figure in local folklore.

The Cailleach was also particularly connected with animals in the role of Lady of the Beasts. In Ireland her favoured animal was the cow and in Scotland her particular animal was the deer. She was known to keep herds of her favourite animals and protect them from hunters, who petitioned her for assistance to be successful in their hunt.

A possibility that must be considered is whether some of the Cailleach tales actually relate to a priestess cult. This process of apotheosis of mythical or historical figures, with their actions assimilated into a divine cult, would blur the boundaries between the Cailleach and her priestesses, were this to be the case. The existence of such a cult is not a new idea, as it was suggested in 1932 by J.G. Mackay in his *The Deer-Cult and the Deer-Goddess Cult of the Ancient Caledonians*. We have found literary references in records from the last two centuries which seem to substantiate the idea of a Cailleach priestess cult of wise women. However, as is often the case these hints ask more questions than they answer, leaving the reader to make up their own mind.

This blurring of boundaries is also seen with regard to other supernatural hag figures found across the British Isles. Some of these have been clearly identified with the Cailleach, such as Nicneven and Gyre Carling. Others such as Black Annis and the Old Woman of the Mountain share a number of motifs and may be derived from the Cailleach. Whilst this is an opinion we subscribe to, we have again presented the evidence for the reader to draw their own conclusions.

We hope that the material we present here helps foster a greater understanding of the origins and importance of the Cailleach, and that it will inspire others, in turn, to further investigate and expand on the knowledge we have today.

Sorita d'Este & David Rankine
    Latha na Caillich 2009
    Powys, Wales

CHAPTER 1

ORIGINS SET IN STONE

The Cailleach stands alone, distinct from the pantheon of Celtic gods, an ancient hag goddess who shaped the land through her control of the forces of nature. She seldom participated in the sagas and legends of the other gods, with her legends focusing on her and her interactions with the land, animals and humanity. As she was not part of the genealogy of any of the families of Celtic gods, we must delve deeper to uncover her roots, and in so doing explore her powers, roles and influences.

The European Origins of the Cailleach

One would perhaps expect to find the first clues about the Cailleach somewhere in the British Isles, but this is not the case at all. The first time she is mentioned in writing is in the classic work *Histories*, written in the fifth century BCE (from 431-425 BCE) by the Greek Historian Herodotus. He mentioned a Celtic tribe on the Iberian peninsula of Spain called the Kallaikoi.

Several centuries later, the Greek geographer Strabo, also referred to this tribe in his famous seventeen volume work *Geography* (produced in the period 7 BCE -23 CE), writing that the women of the Callaeci (who subsequently became the *Galecians*), the Astures and the Cantabri tribes which had recently been conquered by the Romans were particularly ferocious and courageous. Strabo famously declared that they would rather kill their children than allow them to be taken as captives by the Romans, and that they were very hard-working, giving birth whilst they toiled in the fields.

The Roman author Pliny also mentioned the Callaeci in his thirty-seven volume encyclopaedia, *Natural History* in 77 CE. Strabo and Pliny wrote in Latin rather than Greek, so the Kallaikoi of Herodotus became the Calliachi or Callaeci, a name which has been suggested as meaning *worshippers of the Cailleach*.[1] If this is right then it implies that the worship of the Cailleach dates back at least two and a half thousand years to Spain, and was worshipped as a goddess then, possibly as the tutelary goddess of the Callaeci tribe.

The Romans named the province where they found the Callaeci after them, calling it Callaecia meaning *the land of the Callaeci*. This area subsequently became Gallaecia, and hence Galicia, as it is today. Pliny mentioned a number of places there in his work, including the city and port of Cale. The port was called Portus Cale, which was shortened to Portucale, later becoming Portugal in the twelfth century. So the name of this European country actually derives from that of the Cailleach!

---

[1] See e.g. *Ptolemy's 'Callaecia' and the language(s) of the 'Callaeci'*, Luján, 2000 & *Curiosities across the Atlantic: a brief summary of some of the Irish-Galician classical folkloric similarities nowadays. Galician singularities for the Irish*, Paredes, 2000.

From Spain to Ireland

Here we must turn our attention to some of the Irish texts, as there are clear indications of the connection between Spain and Ireland contained within them. The eleventh century text *Leabhar Gabhala Érenn* (*Book of Invasions*), which drew on earlier tales, described the waves of invasions of Ireland by successive mythological peoples like the Fir Bolgs and the Tuatha De Danann. The final wave of invaders of Ireland was the Milesians or Sons of Mil. The Milesians have been identified with the Galecians, resulting in a blending of history and myth in this epic text. The more recent archaeological and genetic evidence does make it clear that the Irish Celts migrated from the Iberian peninsula, so the tales do record historical events, though not with historical accuracy.[2]

The Irish texts perpetuated the beliefs recorded two centuries earlier in the Welsh monk Nennius' eighth/ninth century CE *Historia Brittonum* (*History of Britain*), which recorded *"Long after this, the Scots arrived in Ireland from Spain."*[3] This also makes the significant point that Scotland would become dominated by the Irish Gaels. The Irish started settling on the west coast of Scotland around 350 CE, and by the mid ninth century dominated the country.

Looking at the two distinct Celtic linguistic groups, which are often called P-Celts (sometimes called Brythonic) and Q-Celts (sometimes called Goidelic) also produces significant results. The Q-Celts comprised the

---

[2] See *Did the Irish Come from Spain? The Legend of the Milesians*, Carey, 2001.
[3] *Historia Brittonum* 13, Nennius.

Celts from the Iberian Peninsula (sometimes called Celtiberians), and the Goidelic Celts (Irish, Scottish Gaelic and Manx). As well as the historical evidence and the latest genetic studies, the linguistic evidence also suggests that Celts from Spain did in fact settle Ireland. So based on all these factors, we feel there is a good possibility that they brought the Cailleach with them, and then on to Scotland.

Another pseudo-historical Irish tale, that of *Oisin's Children*,[4] told of how the King of Munster, Owen Mor (Eoghan) fled to Spain, and there married the Princess Beara. When he returned with an army to Ireland, he landed on the island of Bere. He took his bride to the highest hill on the island, and gazing across the peninsula, named the island and the whole Beara peninsula in her honour. Owen Mor was eventually killed by the Irish king Conn of the Hundred Battles, who was supposed to have lived in the period 110-157 CE, giving a second century CE setting for this story. It is easy to see how the connection could be made between the name of the Spanish Princess Beara, the area named after her, and the people she had belonged to – the Callaeci.

The Iberian connection was suggested by Mackenzie in 1915 in his work *Myths of Babylonia and Assyria*. When discussing how Gaelic and Norse stories often have powerful giantesses like Grendel's mother in *Beowulf,* he observed:

> *"It is probable, therefore, that the British stories of female monsters who were more powerful than*

---

[4] Recorded in *Gods and Fighting Men*, Gregory, 1904.

their husbands and sons, are of Neolithic and Iberian origin."[5]

Returning to the *Leabhar Gabhala Érenn*, there is another angle we need to consider implied by this text. As well as the Milesians from Spain, the preceding invaders, the mythical Tuatha De Danann, also deserve our attention. When we follow the journey made by the Tuatha De Danann to invade Ireland, it highlights the other major countries associated with the Cailleach.

The Tuatha De Danann were described as coming from four cities in the north of the world, which at the time would have been Scandinavia. After a period in Greece they travelled to the north of Scotland, from where they invaded Ireland. That the Tuatha De Danann should travel from Scandinavia and then to Scotland and on to Ireland recalls the tales of the Cailleach Bheur arriving in Scotland from Norway, and forming the islands and highlands from stones she carried in her apron. Although this may be coincidental, it is interesting to see that the same document gave all the major countries associated with the Cailleach as part of a series of invasions/migrations of peoples, both north from Spain to Ireland, and south from Norway to Scotland.

A Maltese Origin?

If we look back prior to Herodotus in the fifth century BCE, in search of the earliest origins of the Cailleach, we are left with speculating around the similarities in symbols and motifs in order to find clues. Tracing such

---

[5] *Myths of Babylonia and Assyria*, Mackenzie, 1915.

motifs led us to the legends from Malta regarding the Neolithic megalithic structures there, believed to be the oldest in the world. The Neolithic Ggantija (from the Maltese word meaning *giant*) temples on the island of Gozo were built between 3600-3000 BCE and legend tells us that the temples were built overnight by a giantess called Sansuna. She was also said to have carried the dolmen at Xaghra (also on Gozo) on her head, whilst carrying the supporting stones in her hands.[6] This dolmen has a long history of use as a delivery stone by expectant mothers.

This motif of megalithic structures being built in a very short period of time by a giantess is found repeatedly in stories of the Cailleach. It is thus likely that in these legends from Gozo that we may be looking at a possible early origin for the Cailleach, at the heart of the building of the first known megalithic temple. The builders of the Maltese temples disappeared without a trace around 2300 BCE, so we can only speculate as to what happened to their knowledge and beliefs subsequently. It is very tempting to suggest that some of the Maltese temple builders may have travelled across the Mediterranean and settled in Spain, taking their legends with them.

The Irish Manuscripts

A problem we encountered in tracking the Cailleach's path through history and across different nations is that most of the material we have available was recorded in the last two centuries, with only some Irish stories dating to an earlier time. The first tale which specifically named

---

[6] *Prehistoric Medicine in Malta*, Savona-Ventura & Mifsud, 1999.

the Cailleach as she is perceived today was the ninth century *Lament of the Old Woman of Beara.* This tale described her great age, having seen and survived the biblical Flood, lamenting her lost loves and the bleak future left to an old woman with nothing left to look forward to. The fourteenth century *Yellow Book of Lecan* (drawing on earlier sources) went as far as to make her the genetrix of humanity, with her fifty children by seven husbands being the founders of all the tribes of the world. Other stories with an unnamed sovereignty bestowing hag who may well represent the Cailleach include the eleventh century *The Adventure of the Sons of Eochaid Muigmedon* and the fourteenth century *Fitness of Names.*

Many of the Irish accounts were recorded in folklore collections dating from the nineteenth century through to the early twentieth century, and have been carefully preserved by the Irish Folklore Commission.[7] In the case of Scottish and Manx tales, these have largely been passed to us through works from the early nineteenth through to the early twentieth century.[8]

As well as her stories from Scotland, Ireland and the Isle of Man, there are other areas which need to be considered in our search for the Cailleach. Folklore from around England and Wales, Brittany (France) and even

---

[7] *Coimisiún Béaloideasa Éireann*or CBE
[8] Such as Miller's *Scenes and Legends of the North of Scotland* (1835), J.F. Campbell's *Popular Tales of the West Highlands* (1860), J.G. Campbell's *Superstitions of the Highlands & Islands of Scotland* (1900) and *Witchcraft and Second Sight in the Highlands and Islands of Scotland* (1902), Mackenzie's *Wonder Tales from Scottish Myth and Legend* (1917) & Grant's *Myth, Tradition and Story from Western Argyll* (1925); & Harrison's *Mona Miscellany* (1873) and Gill's *A Manx Scrapbook* (1929).

the Island of Jersey all hint at traces of the Cailleach's presence remembered from the distant past, as do place names.

Thus when we see reference in a twelfth century text to an Old Woman's Mound and Old Woman's Well in North Yorkshire in England, we can suggest this may be linked to the Cailleach. Both the well motif and the mound hint at the Cailleach and the place names equating to a meaning of her name all provide strong circumstantial evidence.

Name Connections

To help track down old references which may be derived from the Cailleach, it is necessary to explore the various meanings of her name. The word Cailleach has several meanings, including *old woman, hag, crone, nun* or *veiled one*. The word is originally derived from the Latin word *pallium* meaning *veil* or *cloak*. When the northern Celtic languages experienced a linguistic shift from P-K, the p became a c/k, so *pallium* became *callium*, which became Cailleach (or with a K instead of the C in Ancient Greek).

The different variants of the Cailleach found in different places, despite their similarities, may not all be one being, but rather a class of beings. The process of equation through name and attribute has led to a whole range of supernatural hags in Scotland all being equated. The Scottish word *carlin* or *carling*, means *old woman* or *witch*, and has been directly equated to the word Cailleach for centuries. Thus the character of Gyre Carling, whose name means *biting old woman* has become equated to the Cailleach Bheur, whose name may also be translated as *biting old woman*, and the two have become assimilated and seen as one homogenous being, especially as Gyre Carling was also described in the sixteenth century as a supernatural giantess.

From this juxtaposition we then see how Gyre Carling, who like the Cailleach was described as Queen of the Fairies, should be equated by Walter Scott in *Minstrelsy of the Scottish Border* (1821) with the figure of Nicneven, another giant hag mentioned in the sixteenth century[9] who was also later described as being Queen of the Fairies. As Nicneven means *daughter of Nevis*, referring to the mountain Ben Nevis which is said to be the Cailleach Bheur's home, then this assumption that they are the same being is easy to accept. Likewise Nicneven is described as having nymphs,[10] indicating a watery connection, which is another major Cailleach motif.

"Nicneven and her nymphs, in numbers anew,
With charms from Caitness, and Chanrie in Ross."

The term nymph was previously used many centuries earlier by the Romans both for specific named and unnamed Celtic goddesses. When the epithet was applied to named Celtic goddesses such as Brigantia and Coventina, they were always associated with water, specifically rivers or healing wells or springs. These watery associations are also seen with the Cailleach, in her connection to wells, rivers and lakes (lochs), so we may also view her in this manner.

---

[9] *The Flyting of Dunbar and Kennedy*, Dunbar, 1508
[10] *The Flyting of Montgomery and Polwart*, Montgomery, 1585

Both Gyre Carling and Nicneven were the subject of negative propaganda, with the former being described in the Bannatyne manuscript (1568) as a cannibal, an epithet also applied to the Scottish/English supernatural hag figure of Black Annis. In a society which had its most renowned horror story being about Sawney Bean, a murdering cannibal and his family, this was a very effective way to demonise a folk figure.

Nicneven was described by Richard Franck in *Northern Memoirs* (1821) as *"the Hecate of Scottish necromancy"*, a title which would subsequently be perpetuated by Walter Scott in his writings, leading to many spurious associations in modern pagan works which have failed to appreciate that the use of Hecate's name is allegorical, and that the author was not suggesting they were the same goddess!

Goddess or Spirit?

When considering whether the Cailleach was a deity or a supernatural figure, we would do well to remember the words of the folklorist Donald Mackenzie in his essay *A Highland Goddess* (1912). Commenting on the propitiatory nature of the relationship between the Scots and the gods of the forces of nature, he observed,

> *"The gods and goddesses were never worshipped in the sense that the term worship is understood by us. If they were not given offerings, they were charmed away by the performance of magical ceremonies."*[11]

---

[11] *The Celtic Review*, 1912, vol 7 no 28.

Certain features stand out of the assorted Cailleach legends and may be considered motifs appropriate to her. These are:

1. shaping the land deliberately or accidentally, including the creation of lakes, hills, islands and megalithic constructions;
2. an association with water, through wells, lakes and rivers;
3. an association with the season of winter;
4. gigantic size;
5. her vast age, being one of the first beings;
6. her guardianship of particular animals;
7. her ability to shape-shift to a variety of forms, including maiden, heron and rock;

Additionally a number of the Irish tales juxtapose the pagan Cailleach with Christianity, in a manner which ranges from respect to belittlement. The tales told of the Cailleach can be seen as exemplifying the spiritual mindset, and changes therein, of the peoples of Britain, especially those of Scotland and Ireland. From being viewed as a benevolent pagan giantess who shaped the land, she became seen as a neutral figure by the early Christians, respected as part of the process of natural development, only to be demonized as time passed and Christianity became ever more rigid and unilateral.

The Different Names of the Cailleach

There are stories and folklore about many different Cailleachs, with different names and titles, many of whom are named for being associated with a particular place or region. They include the Irish Cailleach Béarra (*the Cailleach of Béarra*), the Manx Caillagh ny Gyoamagh (*the Cailleach of Gloominess*) and Caillagh ny Gueshag (Cailleach of the spells), and the many found in Scotland, i.e. Cailleach Bheur or Beira (*the sharp Cailleach*), Cailleach Mhore (*the Great Cailleach*), Cailleach Mhor A Chilibric (*the Great Cailleach of Cilibrich*), Cailleach Mhor Nam Fiadh (*the Great Cailleach of the Deer*), Cailleach na Mointeach (*Cailleach of the Moors*), and Cailleach Beinn Na Bric (*Cailleach of Speckled Mountain*).

The number of different titles given to the Cailleach leads us to the obvious conclusion that she had many regional names, or that the name *Cailleach* was applied to a class of supernatural being, like the hooded Genii Cucullati of Romano-Celtic engravings. Thus it is not surprising to see the term Cailleachan (*old women*) used, though it is in more recent use, such as in Florence McNeill's *The Silver Bough* (1957):

> "*and the Cailleachan or storm hags, who together represent the elemental forces of nature, particularly in a destructive aspect.*"[12]

The Possibility of a Priestess Cult

Indeed, when we consider the apparent migration of the Cailleach with some tribal groups, such as the Celtiberians from Galicia, or from Norse influence down into Scotland, we can speculate as to whether this class of supernatural old women may in fact have had its roots in an old priesthood, transmitting a line of magical

---

12 *The Silver Bough*, McNeill, 1957.

knowledge and representing an early goddess, possibly the Cailleach.

If we revisit the Cailleach motifs, we see a combination of attributes which are clearly supernatural and others which could represent the roles of priesthood. The land shaping stories combine events on a scale beyond human, such as formation of major landscape features, with human endeavours such as megalithic constructions. The association with water, such as guarding wells, was seen for the cults of healing deities in the Celtic world, and as we will demonstrate, is an area which does provide some startling evidence in support of the theory of a priesthood.

The association with winter is an association with natural forces in keeping with a supernatural being or beings. Although gigantic size was often seen as indicating a god or divine nature in the Celtic world, there are also references to large stature which do hint at a priestess cult and could have been exaggerated with time.

The Cailleach's age could indicate either the antiquity of her being, or of a cult worshipping her, transmitting knowledge down the centuries. Also the priestesses would be old (Cailleachan) if their training took a very long time, like the twenty years to become a druid recorded by Julius Caesar around 50-40 BCE in his *Commentaries on the Gallic Wars*.[13]

In his provocative essay *The Deer-Cult and the Deer-Goddess Cult of the Ancient Caledonians*, Mackay argued convincingly that there was a priestess cult associated with the deer in ancient Scotland. Looking at his

---

[13] *Commentaries on the Gallic Wars*, Caesar, VI.14.

evidence, some of the information actually gives an identity to this cult, which is the Cailleach Mhor Nam Fiadh, or rather Cailleachan. The giant women who protected the deer are the woman of Jura, connected with the Cailleach Mhor Nam Fiadh:

> "A group called the Seven Big Women of Jura occur in two of Campbell's tales........ I have already referred to a tale, probably from Badenoch, where a witch refers to the cruelty of her 'sisterhood.' Such a sisterhood or group of witches can only be a group of deer-priestesses, and they imply a corresponding group of goddesses (sic), whose official representatives they were."[14]

This reference to an ancient cult is continued in his essay, when he observed:

> "Island of Eigg.[15] Still called 'Eilean nam Ban Mora' i.e. the Isle of the Big Women. A little loch, with some prehistoric building or crannog constructed in it, is called 'Loch nam Ban Mora' ... The crannog was inhabited by women of such unique proportions that the stepping stones by which they gained their home were set so far apart as to be useless to anyone else. Thus says one tradition. Another tradition says that St. Donann was martyred by the 'Amazon Queen'[16] who reigned in the island; the Queen in question can hardly be anything but the condensation of a group."[17]

---

[14] *The Deer-Cult and the Deer-Goddess Cult of the Ancient Caledonians*, Mackay, 1932.
[15] An island in the Hebrides off the western coast of Scotland.
[16] St Donann was martyred by a Pictish Queen in 617 CE, burned to death with 150 other Christians on the Isle of Eigg.
[17] *The Deer-Cult and the Deer-Goddess Cult of the Ancient Caledonians*, Mackay, 1932.

The final motif of shapeshifting has interesting connotations, as the wearing of animal and bird skins by priesthoods around the world is well documented through the ages. The idea of an old woman transforming into a maiden could easily be seen in view of experienced older priestesses and neophytes at the beginning of their training.

We will present evidence through the book which shows that the idea of a priestess cult is actually far more plausible than has generally been credited. Although this evidence is largely circumstantial, it does suggest an intriguing possibility that has been largely overlooked by history.

CHAPTER 2

EARTH SHAPER

"Determined now her tomb to build,
Her ample skirt with stones she filled,
And dropped a heap on Carron-more;
Then stepped one thousand yards to Loar,
And dropped another goodly heap;
And then with one prodigious leap,
Gained carrion-beg; and on its height
Displayed the wonders of her might."[18]

Foremost amongst the roles taken by the Cailleach in the surviving legends are those of her shaping the landscape and being otherwise directly associated with it. From mountains and caves to lakes and rivers, many features of the British Isles have been both named after, and reputedly shaped by, the Cailleach or Cailleachan.

This is especially conspicuous in Scotland, where many parts of the landscape were said to be created directly and indirectly by the Cailleach. There are also stories from Ireland and the Isle of Man which tell of how features in the environment come from the deeds of the Cailleach. The age of the Cailleach and her old appearance reflect the age of the Earth, the unimaginable spread of years since the birth of our planet. Her age is

---

[18] Jonathan Swift (1667-1745).

often stressed in stories, as is her role in shaping the landscape itself, the latter linking her intimately with the Earth, and also providing perhaps a reassuring continuity back to the unimaginable distance of the far past.

There are stories from parts of England, especially Yorkshire near the Scottish border, which have sufficient points of commonality with Cailleach stories to suggest they also were at one time associated with the Cailleach. Other tales come from places like Wales, Jersey and Brittany, which were all P-Celtic (Brythonic) rather than Q-Celtic (Goidelic). It is clearly significant that such areas should have occasional stories with some common motifs which are possibly connected to the Cailleach, rather than named Cailleach stories. This division suggests that in the distant past there were similarities in the legends, which varied with time and migration, and that she and/or her priesthood (if one existed) were far more associated with the Q-Celtic tribal groups.

Irrespective of divisions, the theme of the giantess with her apron of stones is a common one in British folklore. Likewise there are some tales where it was the devil with an apron of stones whose apron-strings break. Considering the similarity of the two themes, it is impossible not to wonder whether the latter are stories which were adapted by the church to replace indigenous supernatural creatures with the devil, to stamp its mark in a way that retained some of the flavour of the tale, in the same way that churches were built on old sacred sites.

Although the land-forming myths are clearly associated with supernatural beings and not the human figures of priestesses, it is worth noting that there are several myths connecting the building of castles, towers and roads, all of which have known human provenance that was forgotten, giving rise to myths.

1. The Cailleach in Scotland

Ailsa Craig

A piece of local folklore with an amusing bawdy twist was recorded by Eleanor Hull in her article *Legends and Traditions of the Cailleach Bheara or Old Woman (Hag) of Beare* (1927) and subsequently reproduced by Lewis Spence in *The Minor Traditions of British Mythology* (1948).

The tale goes that one day a (French) sailor sailed his boat between the Cailleach's legs as she waded across the ocean carrying her apron load of rocks, with the sail brushing her inner thigh. The surprise touch to an intimate area caused her to drop some of the rocks with a start, forming the Scottish island of Ailsa Craig.

How Loch Awe was Formed

The formation of Loch Awe combines a number of the motifs commonly associated with the Cailleach. She has her herd of goats, she guards a well which she caps and uncaps, and she turns into a stone at the end of it after having inadvertently caused the formation of a loch (lake). The tale is found in early twentieth century works like Mackenzie's *Wonder Tales from Scottish Myth and Legend* (1917) and Grant's *Myth, Tradition and Story from Western Argyll* (1925). However reference to the story is seen in earlier works, such as in Leslie's *The Early Races of Scotland and Their Monuments* (1868), which also credits the Cailleach with the formation of Loch Eck in Cowal.

The story begins by explaining that the Cailleach particularly enjoyed roaming across the land with her herd of goats. Every morning she would remove the large capstone from the well on the summit of Ben Cruachan (in Argyll) to let the water flow. This kept the surrounding lands fertile and provided water for all who needed it.

After she had removed the capstone, which was too large and heavy for anyone else to lift, she would travel across the mountains, driving her herd of magical goats before her. In the evening the Cailleach would return with her herd, and put the capstone back on the well, staunching the flow of water and preventing it from flooding the countryside.

On one such night, when she was weary from driving her goats across the mountains, the Cailleach fell asleep at the side of the well and forgot to replace the capstone. Without her strength and vigilance, there was nobody else to replace the stone and stop the flow of water out of the well. The water gushed forth, breaking through the hills below at the Pass of Bransder. The torrent of water drowned all the local people and cattle in its wake, and finally stopped to form Loch Awe.

Horrified by her mistake and all the deaths she had inadvertently caused, the Cailleach turned to stone in her mourning, her penitent form echoing that of the stone she had forgotten to replace.

How the Ross-shire Hills were Formed

This tale is a classic example of the motif of the breaking apron/basket associated with the Cailleach's formation of land features. It was recorded in Miller's *Scenes and Legends of the North of Scotland* (1835), and it is interesting to see the context that the Cailleach was set into, being linked to Gog-Magog and other giants.

In the distant past the British Isles were ruled by tribes of giants. In the north, in the highlands of Scotland, in what is now Ross-shire, lived such a tribe of giant beings. This primeval tribe was renowned for their strength, and was famous for its incredible kinsfolk, such as Gog-Magog and the Cailleach-Mhore (Great Cailleach). This Cailleach was famed for her strength, even amongst this mightily-hewed tribe.

One day, Cailleach Mhore was walking over the hills with a pannier of earth and rocks on her back. Pausing for breath, she stopped and stood on the site of Ben-Vaichard. As she stood gazing around her, the pannier gave way and all its contents came pouring out. Amidst the noise and chaos the Cailleach-Mhore cursed as her load was scattered. When the dust had cleared her gaze passed over a completely new landscape, with new hills formed by the earth and rocks she had been carrying.

Nessa's Lament

Nestled in the tale of Beira and Bride in Mackenzie's *Wonder Tales from Scottish Myth and Legend* (1917) is a tale which explains how Loch Ness was formed through the anger of the Cailleach. There is a parallel here to one of the tales recorded in the twelfth century Irish *Dindshenchas* (*History of Places*) about the Morrigan, who turns a maiden called Odras into a pool of water in her anger. In that instance the maiden allowed a bull to mate with one of the cows in the Morrígan's supernatural cow herd.

The Cailleach had two wells in Inverness-shire which she had to cap and open every day. Tired of spreading her efforts, she hired a maiden to remove the smaller cap of this well at sunrise in the morning and replace it at sunset. This maid, whose name was Nessa, was late reaching the well one night, and as she approached she saw the water flowing furiously from the well towards her. Nessa ran for her life, leaving the well uncapped.

The Cailleach saw this from the top of Ben Nevis, and furiously cursed Nessa for neglecting her duty. For running from the water she cursed her to run forever and never leave water. Nessa was transformed into a river and Loch, which is where the river Ness and Loch Ness come from.

Once every year, on the anniversary of her transformation, Nessa is said to emerge from the loch in her maiden form and sing a beautiful sad song to the moon, lamenting her misfortune. The song is said to be more beautiful than any other melody you could ever hear.

Carlin Maggie & other Carlin Stones

Carlin Maggie is the name of a place in Scotland based on local folklore.[19] While the figure of Carlin Maggie was the head witch of a coven and not specifically

---

[19] Recounted in *Examples of Printed Folk-lore Concerning Fife with Some Notes on Clackmannan and Kinross-shire,* Simpkins, 1914.

connected to the Cailleach, the theme of her being transformed to stone, and the interconnection of the words Carlin and Cailleach made it worth inclusion as the possible survival of an earlier tale.

Carlin Maggie was with her witches one day when she saw the devil approaching with a load of rocks. Maggie flyted[20] the devil and then fled, chased by him, after he dropped his stones on Bishops Hill (where they became known as *The Devil's Burden*). Angered by her flyting, the devil turned Maggie into a pillar of stone on the slope overlooking Lochleven, where she still stands today. The pillar of stone bears her name, Carlin Maggie.

The name Carlin is applied to other stones in Scotland too. A large boulder near Dunlop in North Ayrshire is known as the Carlin's Stone. Another large stone near Waterside in East Ayrshire is called the Carlin Stone, with nearby watercourses which run into the river Irvine called the Carlin Burn, Hag Burn and Hags Burn.[21] A third Carlin Stone forms part of a ruined stone circle at Backhill of Drachlaw in Aberdeenshire.

As well as stones there are several places in Scotland with the name Carlin where the associated folklore has been lost or not recorded. These are the mountain Carlin's Cairn in north-west Kirkcudbrightshire, and Carlinwark, a loch to the south of Castle Douglas also in Kirkcudbrightshire; Carlin Skerry, a rocky islet in the south of Orkney; and Carlin Tooth, a summit in the

---

[20] Flyting is a form of insulting, usually performed as a contest and sometimes in rhyme. The Cailleach is associated with Flyting through Nicneven and Gyre Carling, who are mentioned in *The Flyting of Dunbar and Kennedy* (1508) and *The Flyting of Montgomery and Polwart* (1585).
[21] A Burn is a watercourse, which may vary in size from a large stream to a small river.

Cheviot Hills in Roxburghshire close to the English border.[22]

Cailleach na Mointeach

There are other stones which have Cailleach associations as well. To the south of the stone circle of Callanais (Callanish) on the Scottish isle of Lewis is a stone which resembles a reclining figure. This stone is known as Cailleach na Mointeach (*the Cailleach of the Moors*), and her proximity to this major stone circle again indicates her significance in connection with the landscape from ancient times.

This stone has an astronomical connection, as the Callanish Stones were used for lunar observation. Every eighteen years the full moon rises between her knees, giving the impression that the Cailleach stone is giving birth to the moon.[23]

This is not the only standing stone attributed to the Cailleach. In Uist in Ireland are the two stones known as *Leac nan Calileacha Dubba*, (*the Stones of the Black Hags*), and atop the Moher Cliffs is the stone known as the Hag's Head. This also leads us to speculate about other stones which have creation legends associated with hags, witches and supernatural female figures, like Long Meg and her daughters at Little Salkeld in Cumbria.

---

[22] *Ordnance Gazetteer of Scotland*, Groome, 1896.
[23] *Callanish: the Stones, and Moon, and the Sacred Landscape*, Curtis & Curtis, 1994.

2. The Cailleach in Ireland

The Shower of Stones

Any wise person knows you should not get between two arguing giants, as they have a habit of throwing boulders and large stones, and this can be clearly seen in the fight that took place in Ireland between two Cailleachs. [24]

In the distant past, an argument broke out in the parish of Magh Cuilinn between the Cailleach Béarra and another Cailleach, whose name has been lost to posterity. Suffice it to say that they argued to such a degree that they could find no common ground, and they agreed to resolve their differences with a boulder throwing contest!

The two Cailleachs grimly gathered up piles of rocks on the top of the two hillocks on top of the Poll Mountain one evening to use as ammunition the next day in their stone-throwing contest. They rose early and started pelting each other with stones, exchanging cries as the missiles struck skin and bone. Both became bruised and cut from the damage they did to each other with the barrage of stones.

As the contest continued, the Cailleach Béarra had a realization, and cunningly started throwing her rocks beyond the other Cailleach, deliberately missing her. The other Cailleach seized her chance and threw all her rocks at the Cailleach, hurting her greatly with her frenzied throws and raising many a cry of pain from the Cailleach Béarra.

After a while, when all the other Cailleach's rocks were gone, she looked around in horror. There were no

---

[24] CBE 74:22-24

stones or boulders near her, and the Cailleach Béarra was left surrounded by a large pile of rocks.

At this point the Cailleach Béarra seized the moment, and systematically pelted the other Cailleach with these, beating her into a pile of bones with her well aimed throws.

When the locals arrived later in the day they found the Cailleach Béarra stretched out on top of one hillock and bleeding profusely from her injuries. Of the other Cailleach there was no sign, as she had been buried under the pile of rocks thrown by the Cailleach Béarra. The rocks thrown by the other Cailleach have long since been swallowed by the marshy land lower down, leaving only the cairn as a memorial to the dead Cailleach and the wisdom of the Cailleach Béarra.

This story raises an interesting point about the nature of the Cailleach. This tale has a second Cailleach fighting with the Cailleach Béarra, indicating that the name *Cailleach* refers not to a singular unique being, but to a class of being instead. This in turn then brings into question the nature of the Cailleach, for if the name refers to a class of powerful or otherwise supernatural beings, instead of to a particular deity, then it sheds a different type of light on it. Perhaps, as Anne Ross suggests, we should rather think of them as:

> *"great supernatural hags haunting mountain passes or driving their deer over the hills and conferring benefits and evils on humanity as they saw fit."*[25]

---

[25] *Pagan Celtic Britain*, Ross, 1967.

Examining the main roles associated with the various Cailleachs in the different stories, guardianship is a recurrent theme. We see her guarding wells and guarding animals, and controlling the elemental forces of nature such as the weather, water and earth.

The Hag's Chair

Locals around Sliabh na Caillighe (*the Hill of the Witch*) near Loughcrew in County Meath tell of how the Cailleach Béarra formed the cairn complex there by dropping stones from her apron. Of these, the throne-shaped boulder known as the Hag's Chair is perhaps the best known and most specifically associated with her.

The story goes[26] that one day the Cailleach Béarra came down from the north to perform a spell which would give her great power if it worked. She had to make four cairns each a mile apart by jumping from hill to hill and dropping stones from her apron. Filling her apron with stones, the Cailleach Béarra began her spell.

She dropped a cairn on Carnbane, and with a mighty leap jumped a mile to the summit of Sliabh na Caillighe, dropping a second cairn of stones including a large throne-shaped boulder. A third leap took her to another hill a mile distant, where she dropped her third cairn. As she made her final leap to claim the power of her spell, she slipped and fell in the town of Patrickstown and broke her neck. The mournful locals buried her in a field to the east of the town, in a field called Cul a'mhota (*Back of the Mote*), but this has since been destroyed and lot to antiquity.

---

[26] As described in *Legends and Traditions of the Cailleach Bheara or Old Woman (Hag) of Beare*, Hull, 1927.

Meelick Round Tower

Another local tale tells of how the Cailleach Béarra was interrupted building Meelick Round Tower outside Swinford in County Mayo.[27] Originally the tower was part of a monastery, but like St Michael's Tower on Glastonbury Tor, the tower is the only part of the structure that remains.

The story goes that the Cailleach Béarra was building the tower to the sky, like a Tower of Babel. However she was interrupted by a passing boy who made a rude comment which caused her to jump down angrily. The boy commented that he could see her arse, and she jumped down, abandoning the tower and leaving the marks from her knees in the rocks below where she landed.

3. The Cailleach in England

Although there are no specific myths in England which name the Cailleach, there are places with names which equate to a translation of her name and which have appropriate motifs such as well or standing stone. Additionally, in some places there is local folklore which is suggestive of her. As a result we can speculate as to possible connections when examining the themes expressed, particularly the formation of megalithic chambers with huge stones which are ascribed to witches and spinsters, who can both be linked to her through their magic and age.

---

[27] CBE 17:12-13.

Kerlingkelde

A site that is clearly linked to the Cailleach is the Old Woman's Well at Guisborough in North Yorkshire. The well is now lost, though it was referred to in the *Guisborough Cartulary*, a twelfth century work, as Kerlingkelde.[28] The name Kerlingkelde comes from the Scottish word *Carling* which as we have already mentioned means *old woman* or *witch* – hence *old woman's well*. There was also an Old Woman's Mound (Kerling Hou or Carling Howe) in the area which has also been lost.

Wade's Wife's Causeway

The old Roman road which ran from Malton across the moors to Whitby on the coast in Yorkshire was subsequently ascribed to the giant Wade, best known as the father of the smith god Weland. Local folklore, forgetting the Roman origins of the road, came up with the following tale about the road, which is known as Wade's Causeway or Wade's Wife's Causeway. Every day Wade's wife, the giantess Bell, herded their cows over the moor, so the couple decided to build a road to make the daily journey easier. Bell carried the stones in her apron, and on a couple of occasions the apron strings broke, leaving piles of stones on the moor.

The giantess dropping stones from her apron after the strings break is a common Cailleach motif, leading us to wonder whether her influence has not entered this local tale. Also Wade, whose mother was a sea giantess,

---

[28] See *The Place-Names of the North Riding of Yorkshire*, Smith, 1928.

was taught healing by a wild woman, which also hints at a Cailleach connection entering the story.

The Devil's Chair

The Stiperstones in Shropshire are connected with a range of local folklore. They were stolen from the devil by a giantess after his apron-strings broke scattering stones, but he then made her apron-strings break casing the five stones to scatter. However the stones dropped by the giantess were connected with a prophecy, which said that if the stones sank into the earth then England would come to ruin. The devil frequently visits the stones to try and force them into the earth so he can claim all the souls in England, and sits on the stone called the Devil's Chair, trying to force it into the earth.[29]

Another tale says that all the ghosts of Shropshire and the surrounding counties gather on the longest night (i.e. the night before the Winter Solstice, so usually the 20th or 21st December) to elect their king for the coming year.[30] This again hints at the Cailleach, with the stones dropped by a giantess and also being associated with sovereignty.

Other Stones

There is a stone called the Old Woman near Cornholme in West Yorkshire. Also in the north of England is a standing stone called the Old Woman on Bamford Moor in Derbyshire.[31] Both of these stones may

---

[29] *English Folktales*, Keding & Johnson, 2005.
[30] *Collecteana Archaeologica* Vol 1, Wright, 1843.
[31] *The History and Gazetteer of the County of Derby*, Noble, 1831.

be associated with the Cailleach, as a translation of the word Cailleach itself.

The Queen of the Fairies Chair near Lowgill in Lancashire has a suggestive name, being mindful of the attribution of the Cailleach as queen of the fairies.

Chambers

Other examples of sites which may be connected to the Cailleach include Kit's Coty House in Kent and Spinster's Rock in Devon.

Kit's Coty House in Kent is a megalithic chamber tomb said to have been raised by three witches, with a fourth witch adding the capstone. The first record of the name dates to 1576, so any earlier associations are unknown.[32]

Spinster's Rock in Devon is the remains of an ancient burial chamber which legend tells us was raised by three spinsters before breakfast on their way to the market.[33]

4. The Cailleach in Wales

The site of the chambered tombs at Barclodiad y Gawres (*the Giantess's Apron*) near Caernarfon Bay on the west coast of Wales hints at a connection with the Cailleach. The story goes that a giantess dropped the stones there when hearing how much further she had to carry the stones to build her home on Anglesey, which is of course very reminiscent of the stories associated with the Cailleach.[34]

---

[32] *The Penny Cyclopædia* Vol III: Athanaric – Bassano; 1835.
[33] *The Monthly Magazine* Vol 26:2, 1808.
[34] *Ainsworths Magazine* Vol 15, 1849.

5. The Cailleach on the Isle of Man

The Caillagh ny Gyoamagh's Slip

In the Isle of Man, the Cailleach was well known to the locals under the name of Caillagh ny Gyoamagh, or Lady of Gloominess. This title reflects her disposition, as her mood could be as gloomy as a rain storm, or grey as a storm cloud.

The Caillagh ny Gyoamagh was said to reside in Cronk yn Irree Lhaa, meaning the *Hill of the Day-rise*. One day the Caillagh took a giant stride from Barrule hill on the south of the Island. She had been visiting the sea god Manannan Beg Mac y Leirr (*Little Manannan son of the Sea*), who lived there and was returning home. However she slipped and fell into a crevice, and her heel left its mark as she tried to stop herself falling, which can be seen to this day and bears her name, Caillagh ny Gyoamagh.[35]

A similar tale is told in Kidalton parish, Islay, in Scotland. A hill called Beinn na Caillich (*Hill of the Old Woman*) is named after her, being the reputed burial place of a giantess in the days of the hero Finn, and a furrow down its side called Sgrìoh na Caillich was said to be made by her as she slid down it in a sitting position.[36]

The Falling Rocks

Another tale from the Isle of Man described how the Witch of Man (i.e. the Caillagh ny Gyoamagh) was flying over Glenfernate carrying a huge rock in her apron. She

---

[35] *A Manx Scrapbook*, Walter, 1929.
[36] *A Tour in Scotland and Voyage to the Hebrides 1772*, Pennant, 1776.

intended to use the rock as part of a castle she was building for the Great Comyn of Banedach.[37] As she flew over a devout Christian gamekeeper, he exclaimed "God preserve us", at which her apron-strings broke and the rock fell to the ground near Kirkmichael. The Caillagh could not find another apron-string as strong to replace the one that had broken and so she abandoned her castle-building.

6. The Cailleach in Jersey

In Jersey the giantess figure of the Cailleach was replaced by (or equated to) fairies, who frequently carried stones in their aprons in a similar manner. This can be seen in the legends associated with a number of ancient monuments.[38]

A site which was said to have been formed by fairies is Le Clios des Tres Pierres near St Ouen's Pond. The three menhirs were supposedly brought in their aprons by three fairies long ago and deposited there to frighten the Turks and discourage invasion. The large slab of unknown purpose called La Table des Marthes (The Witnesses' Table) at La Corbière was another stone said to have been carried by fairies.

Le Ville-ès-Nouaux at St Andrews Park and Le Pouquelaye de Faldouët (the fairystone of Faldouët) are burial chambers which were also said to have been transported by fairies in their aprons.

---

[37] The Fairies in Tradition and Literature, Briggs, 1967.
[38] The Megalith Builders, Ford, nd.

7. The Cailleach in Brittany

Other possible giantess/fairy with apron sites are seen by moving across the English Channel to Brittany. A site named after a giant is Le Tombeau de la Groac'h Ahès (*the Tomb of the Fairy Ahès*), near Cavan, with Ahès being the giant's name. Also in Brittany is Le Tombeau de la Groac'h Rouge (*the Tomb of the Red Fairy*) near Prat in Côtes du Nord. This site was reputedly carried there by a red fairy in her apron.[39]

8. The Cailleach in Norway

There is a Scottish tradition cited by Eleanor Hull[40] of the Cailleach Bheur having come from Norway, carrying the stones which formed the Western Isles and the coasts and mountains of the Scottish highlands. From this perspective she continued the Norse tradition of primal giants representing the wild forces of nature. Specifically her qualities duplicated many of those associated with the inhabitants of the Norse world of Jotunheim. Jotunheim is mentioned in the tale of Gefion, and was considered to be home to both the hill/rock giants and the frost/ice giants.

This is one of those many connections needing further exploration between the Norse and Celtic worlds, like the link between the Irish battle goddess the Morrígan and the Norse Valkyries. That the theme of land-shaping is also seen in Norse myths is demonstrated by tales such as that of the Norse goddess Gefion. This

---

[39] *Meg and Her Daughters: Some Traces of Goddess Beliefs in Megalithic Folklore*, Menefee, 1996.
[40] *Legends and Traditions of the Cailleach Bheara or Old Woman (Hag) of Beare*, Hull, 1927.

tale was told in the Norse *Ynglinga Saga*, part of the *Heimskringla* (*Chronicle of the Kings of Norway*) written by Snorri Sturluson in 1225 and said to be based on a ninth century tale. The same story with minor variations was also told by Snorri in the *Gylfaginning* (*The Tricking of Gylfi*), part of the *Prose Edda*.

Gefion and the Creation of Zealand

Gefion, whose name may be translated as *Giving One*, was a goddess of the Æsir. She appeared at the court of the Swedish king Gylfi in disguise and entertained him with her singing. In return the king rewarded her with as much land as she could plough around in a day and night. Gefion then transformed her four giant sons into oxen and with their aid she pulled the Danish island of Zealand out of mainland Sweden.

The gap left by Zealand was filled by lake Malaren in Sweden in its stead, which is why its shape is said to be similar to that of the island of Zealand. The connection between Gefion and giants is emphasized in the story, as the four oxen are said to be her sons from her liaison with a giant in Jotunheim, magically transformed for the purpose of ploughing.

CHAPTER 3

WATER WITCH

Water was viewed as a powerful and liminal force in the Celtic world and featured prominently in many of the legends of the Cailleach. As a water goddess we see her in the role of well guardian, capping and uncapping wells, being magically transformed by water, transforming a maiden into a river and lake, being connected with lakes and whirlpools, and responsible for floods. All of these events and roles highlight her transitional nature and emphasise her as a bringer of change to those she encounters.

The ninth century *Lament of the Old Woman of Beara*, contains the first reference connecting the Cailleach with a flood that she has created:

> *"My flood has guarded well that which was deposited with me; Jesus, Son of Mary, has saved it so that I am not sad up to ebb."*[41]

She goes on to lament how the world has changed since the flood saying:

> *"Today there is scarcely a dwelling-place I would recognise; what was in flood is all ebbing"*

---

[41] *Lament of the Old Woman of Beara*, C9th CE.

Several Scottish stories also connected floods with the Cailleach, such as the formation of Loch Awe and Loch Ness. In the case of the formation of Loch Awe, some versions of the story imply that if the Cailleach neglected to cap the well at night the waters would eventually flood the entire world. This recalls the motif of the Great Flood, which some scholars have associated with her. However the connection made in legends between the Cailleach and the Great Flood is more usually based on an emphasis on her great age, as a survivor of the flood.

The Cailleach Bheur was particularly associated with the Corryvreckan whirlpool, north of the island of Jura on the west coast of Scotland. The name Corryvreckan means *cauldron of plaid*, taken from the legendary use of the whirlpool by the Cailleach to wash her plaid in. It was said that when she had washed her plaid and it was all white, winter was heralded, as implied by the symbolism of the white snow covering the land. The Corryvreckan whirlpool is one of the largest in the world, greatly feared due to its unpredictability and the speed the weather in the surrounding area can change.

Elsewhere in Scotland the Cailleach was believed to control tidal lochs, creating violent storms which would endanger boats whenever the mood took her. The most extreme form of her weather aspect is seen in descriptions of her given by the sixteenth century Scottish poet Dunbar. He described her coming down from Lochlann in a dark cloud whilst throwing down thunderbolts and lightning, which set the forests of Scotland on fire. Her spittle forming Loch Lomond is another water motif which also emphasised her ability to shape the landscape.

"She spittit Lochlomond with her lips; Thunner and fireflaucht[42] flew fae her hips."[43]

The sailors of Cromarty called the Cailleach *"Gentle Annie"*, in an effort to placate her. They perceived the sudden storms in the Forth as being tricks played by the Cailleach who could control the weather and as a result they did their best to remain on her good side. It is noteworthy here that her connection with the sea is further emphasised by her marriage to the Celtic sea god Manannan found in two of the surviving legends, one from Ireland and one from the Isle of Man.

In addition to her ability to control the weather, the Cailleach was also credited with being able to predict the weather, as recounted in the Irish tale of the *Foolish Servant* (CBE 74:14). It is interesting to note that the weather changes she created were usually water related, i.e. rain and storms, reinforcing the notion that she controlled the elemental forces of water. Even the stone named after her in Stralachlan, the Cailleach Vearor Vera (*Old Wife of Thunder*) had storm-bringing qualities attributed to it.

Significantly there is mention of a Cailleach Uisg, meaning *Water Cailleach*, in the folklore gathered together in the *Carmina Gadelica*. This terminology is reminiscent of the name Nicneven in the sixteenth century being associated with water nymphs.

---

[42] Lightning.
[43] *The Manere of the Crying of Ane Playe*, Dunbar, C16.

The healing qualities of wells and springs were common features in the Celtic world, particularly associated with goddesses, such as Coventina and Brigantia. As the priesthood of such goddesses was often based around their holy wells, these enduring features of the landscape may also provide us with some evidence for the worship of the Cailleach, as well as clues of a possible priestess cult dedicated to her.

One example of such a holy spring survives in the Scottish Hebrides islands. Describing the well of Tobar-Rath-Bhuathaig (*the lucky well of Bethag*) on the Hebridean island of Gigha, *The Early Races of Scotland and Their Monuments* (1866) recorded a reference to two crones (i.e. Cailleachan) who possessed the secret knowledge of how to close the fountain properly:

> *"if the fountain were not properly closed, a storm would arise, and the whole island be overwhelmed. The reverend author of the statistical account of the parish in 1792 mentions that two crones, named Galbreath and Graham, were then said to possess the secret, and if required would practice the necessary rites."[44]*

Another reference may be found in *Scottish Folk Lore and Folk Life* (1935) in which the author recounts a story which suggests that the Cailleach, and a possible priesthood dedicated to her, continued well into the twentieth century:

> *"A gamekeeper at Corrour Lodge, Inverness-shire, told my friend Mr Ronald Burn, in 1917, that the*

---

[44] *The Early Races of Scotland and Their Monuments*; Leslie, 1866.

Cailleach of Ben Breck, Lochaber, had cleaned out a certain well, and had afterwards washed herself therein, in that same year. And in 1927 the late Dr Miller of Fort William, Lochaber, informed me that the old Cailleach is still well-known there."[45]

1. Predicting the Weather

The Corryvreckan Whirlpool

For centuries sailors have feared the unpredictable nature of the Corryvreckan whirlpool, telling tales of how it reflected the Cailleach's moods. Traditionally it was claimed that foam or small wavelets meant the Cailleach is treading her laundry, and that if you heard a noise like thunder the Cailleach was sneezing, and you should beware. Both these signs were ones to avoid and avoiding the whirlpool after seeing the foam or hearing the sneeze, would ensure living another day.

The locals described the sounds as being heard for many miles for days before the coming of winter.

"Before the washing the roar of a coming tempest is heard by people on the coast for a distance of twenty miles, and for a period of three days before the cauldron boils. When the washing is over the plaid of old Scotland is virgin white."[46]

The Foolish Servant

The Cailleach Béarra had a young boy for a servant who always thought he knew best. One day he went to shake out the hay without her instruction. The Cailleach chastised him for his foolishness, demanding to know

---

[45] *Scottish Folk Lore and Folk Life,* Mackenzie, 1935.
[46] *Myth, Tradition and Story from Western Argyll* Grant, 1925.

why he went to shake out the hay when it was going to rain within the hour.

Chastened, the boy asked the Cailleach how she could know such a thing. The Cailleach replied that when she was out she heard the scald-crow scream it and the deer speak it (note the deer, her special animal in Scotland). The boy, horrified by her magical ability, crossed himself and said:

> "Heed not the scald-crow nor the deer
> And heed not a woman's words
> Whether it's early or late the sun rises
> The day will be as God wills it."[47]

The Caillagh ny Gyoamagh

On the Isle of Man, folklore associated with the Caillagh ny Gyoamagh clearly indicated her nature as a weather spirit. If St Bride's Day, 1st February, was fine, she would come out to gather sticks to keep her warm for the rest of the summer. If it was wet she would stay in, and had to improve the weather if she wanted to come out. A fine 1st February was therefore a bad omen, unlike in Scotland where it represented the first of the three days borrowed by Angus to rescue Bride from the Cailleach. The Caillagh ny Gyoamagh was sometimes seen in the shape of a giant bird like a heron when she gathered sticks.

2. The Cailleach in the Carmina Gadelica

The Consecration of the Seed (*An Coisrigeadh Sìoil*) in *Carmina Gadelica* ends with a verse mentioning the

---

[47] CBE 74:14.

Cailleach in the same lines as rough storms, suggesting memories of her weather connection. It reads:

> "No Cailleach will come with bad times, To ask a palm bannock from us, What time rough storms come with frowns Nor stint nor hardship shall be on us."[48]

The same book also described the Cailleach Uisg in a manner which is clearly another remnant of older lore. It tells how in the first week of April she switched the grass with her magic wand, keeping down the vegetation until the combination of sun, dew and rain overcome her and she flew off in a rage with the words,

> "It escaped me below, it escaped me above,
> It escaped me between my two hands,
> It escaped me before, it escaped me behind,
> It escaped me between my two eyes.
> It escaped me down, it escaped me up,
> It escaped me between my two ears,
> It escaped me thither, it escaped me hither,
> It escaped me between my two feet.
> I throw my druidic evil wand
> Into the base of a withered hard whin bush,
> Where shall not grow 'fionn' nor 'foinnidh',
> But fragments of grassy 'froinnidh'."

3. Summoning the Water

Some of the stories told in the previous chapter demonstrated the power of the Cailleach to summon water, such as the formation of Loch Ness. This theme is also seen in stories like Dunbar's sixteenth century *The*

---

[48] *Carmina Gadelica*, Carmichael, 1900.

Manere of the Crying of Ane Playe, with her saliva forming Loch Lomond.

The Old Wife of Thunder

In the parish of Stralachlan in Scotland, say the Parish records, was a stone on a hill which bore the name of Cailleach Vearor Vera, or *The Old Wife of Thunder*.[49] This stone, thought to be a manifestation of the Cailleach herself, was believed to have many magical properties. Locals swore the stone could transport itself to any hilltop in the area and it was often seen in unexpected locations. The locals were careful never to upset this stone, for they believed it could command thunder and bring terrible deluges of rain, just like the Cailleach herself.

Another stone named after the Cailleach and with magical powers attributed to it can be found on the Scottish island of Gigha. On the southern tip of the island is Cnoc a'Bhodaich (*the Hill of the Old Man*), topped by two stones known as the Bodach and the Cailleach (*Old Man* and *Hag*). According to local lore the stones have magical powers and walk the heath at night.

Stones with the names of A'Chailleach and Bodach (*Hag* and *Old Man*) are also found on opposite sides of the glen overlooking Loch Eanaich in the Cairngorms in the Highlands of Scotland. These stones were said in local lore to talk to each other across the glen in booming voices.

---

49 *The New Statistical Account of Scotland*, 1845.

CHAPTER 4

CRONE OF WINTER

"O life that ebbs like the seal
I am weary and old, I am weary and old –
Oh! How can I happy be
All alone in the dark and cold.

I'm the old Beira again,
My mantle no longer is green,
I think of my beauty with pain
And the days when another was queen.

My arms are withered and thin,
My hair once golden is grey;
'Tis winter – my reign doth begin –
Youth's summer has faded away.

Youth's summer and autumn have fled –
I am weary and old, I am weary and old.
Every flower must fade and fall dead
When the winds blow cold,
when the winds blow cold."[50]

In the winter months it used to be believed that you might catch a glimpse of the Cailleach, shrouded in white and riding through the sky on the back of a wolf. If you did, you would keep very still for it was widely known that she could bring snow and blizzards, swirling the air

---

[50] Song of the Cailleach Beira, *Wonder Tales from Scottish Myth and Legend*; Mackenzie, 1917

with her magic wand and keeping her mantle of snow over the land. At Samhain[51] she would become dominant and ride through the land on her wolf, striking down signs of growth with her magic wand, spreading snow and winter across the land. She then ruled until the coming of summer at Beltane.[52]

There are regional variations on this story, some of which instead has the Cailleach ruling winter from the Autumn Equinox[53] to the Spring Equinox,[54] i.e. the days when there is more dark than light, and when water and cold tend to dominate the climate. The 25th March, just after the Spring Equinox, was referred to as Latha na Caillich (*Cailleach Day*), and is now sometimes known as *Lady Day*. Interestingly autumn and winter correspond to the elements of Water and Earth respectively, and these are the two elements that she was most associated with, which are also traditionally the two elements perceived as being feminine in nature.

The wintery associations in the story of Beira tie into references in the seasonal cycle. Hence the explanation for the short burst of good weather than often seems to introduce February, and likewise the connection to the wolf, with the old Gaelic name for the month of January being Faoilleach or *wolf month*.

Although the Cailleach as a winter goddess is not found in folklore beyond Britain, on the Continent we find the Germanic winter goddess Frau Holda or Holle. There is a significant number of shared motifs, such as Holda being described as a crone who can also appear as

---

51 Halloween, 1st November.
52 Mayday, 1st May.
53 September 21st/22nd.
54 March 21st/22nd.

a beautiful maiden, and having connections with witches and with water through pools and fountains and other water sources.

Like the local Scottish descriptions of the Cailleach's behaviour for the Corryvreckan whirlpool, Holda's behaviour was said to determine the weather. Thus when it snowed Holda was shaking out her feather pillows, fog was smoke from her fire and thunder was Holda reeling flax. Curiously, like the Cailleach, there was ambivalence towards Holda from the Christian Church which became more negative with time. Thus it seems that certain characteristics were clearly associated with European winter goddesses, as there is no evidence to indicate that Holda and the Cailleach came from the same root source.

As winter marks the end of the year, leading towards its death, it is easy to see why a supernatural figure looking like an old woman should have come to personify the power of winter. The seasonal tides of the year have come to be associated with the ages of human life, and so the spring maiden matures into the old crone of winter, in a cyclical manner reflecting the seasons upon the Earth.

The beauty of the Cailleach reflected the beauty of winter. The lines on her face all told stories, she did not have the wrinkle-free smoothness of a young girl, but rather the wisdom won through age and experience. Her eyes spoke of death, wonder and determination, all of which were found in the harsh snows which blanketed the land and reminded people of their own mortality.

1. Winter Customs

During the harsh winter months, people in the Scottish Highlands would expel death at Christmas by burning a log called the Cailleach Nollaich (or Nollig), a name which means *the old woman of Christmas.* On Christmas Eve the head of the household would go out and find a tree stump, which he would roughly carve in the shape of an old woman. This would then be burned on the fire whilst everyone made jokes and when the log had burned the festivities could start.[55] This was believed to keep the angel of death from the household for the next year, showing another Pagan-Christian synergy in folk practice.

Another apotropaic winter custom regarding the Cailleach from the Scottish Highlands is that of *Calluinn,* on New-Year's Eve (31st December). The hide of a winter cow would be wrapped around one man's head, and the rest of the men would strike it with switches. The unruly procession would circle around each house in the village three times *deiseal* (sunwise) all the while banging on the walls and singing, or perhaps shouting:

> *"The calluinn of the yellow bag of hide,*
> *Strike the skin (upon the wall)*
> *An old wife [Cailleach] in the graveyard*
> *An old wife in the corner*
> *Another old wife beside the fire,*
> *A pointed stick in her two eyes,*
> *A pointed stick in her stomach,*
> *Let me in, open this."*[56]

---

[55] *History of the West Highlands,* MacCulloch, 1924.
[56] *Witchcraft and Second Sight in the Highlands and Islands of Scotland,* Campbell, 1902.

Each of the revellers would then have to repeat a rhyme, and after the leader of the revellers had presented the head of the household with a *caisein-uchd*, the party would be admitted and offered food and drink. The caisein-uchd was a strip of sheepskin from the breast of a sheep wrapped around a stick. This had to be singed in the fire, passed three times around the family and held to the noses of all of them. Following this the drinks could be consumed, which would inevitably be whisky. This, it was believed, would bring protection for the entire household for the whole of the coming year. The parallels of symbolism within and without the house and the threefold movement sunwise, as well as the rhymes, all appear in folk customs around the British Isles in a variety of forms.

A further Scottish custom demonstrated the winter connection of the Cailleach in relation to the interplay of the two original seasons of the year, those of summer and winter. Located in Glen Calliche, off Glen Lyon, is Tigh nam Bodach (*The Hag's House*). This small dry stone structure contained water-shaped stones known as the *Cailleach and her children*. In the summer months, from May 1st – November 1st, the stones were placed outside the shrine, upon the advent of winter the local shepherd took them into the shrine, where they were kept until the next summer.

2. The Cailleach and Bride

All around Scotland the tale was told in many variant forms, of how the Cailleach Beira captured the summer maiden Bride, and held her prisoner in her mountain hall, beneath Ben Nevis, the tallest mountain in

Scotland. The different elements of this tale were brought together and told by Donald Mackenzie in his book *Wonder tales from Scottish Myth and Legend* (1917).

The Cailleach's appearance was said to reflect the bleakness of winter. Her skin was blue-black, like a winter storm cloud, her white hair looked like twigs covered in frost, and her single eye glared out at the world like the winter sun. The Cailleach was a harsh mistress, and kept the beautiful princess Bride captive.

Bride was given the hardest and most menial tasks to perform. One day Beira gave Bride a brown fleece to wash, insisting she washed it in the nearby stream until it went completely white. Bride washed the fleece, but it never went white. One day as she washed the fleece in a pool she was approached by an old man, who took pity on her. He shook the mantle three times and the mantle turned white as snow. He told her he was Father Winter and gave her some snowdrops.

> *"Said Father Winter: 'If Beira scolds you, give her these flowers, and if she asks where you found them, tell her that they came from the green rustling fir-woods. Tell her also that the cress is springing up on the banks of streams, and that the new grass has begun to shoot up in the fields.'"*

Bride returned to the cave and was scolded by Beira when she saw the snowdrops. Bride repeated what she had been told, causing Beira to fly into a fury.

> *"Beira summoned her eight hag servants, and spoke to them, saying: 'Ride to the north and ride to the south, ride to the east and ride to the west, and I will ride forth also. Smite the world with frost and tempest, so that no flower may bloom and no*

grass blade survive. I am waging war against all growth.'

When she had spoken thus, the eight hags mounted on the backs of shaggy goats and rode forth to do her bidding. Beira went forth also, grasping in her right hand her black magic hammer. On the night of that very day a great tempest lashed the ocean to fury and brought terror to every corner of the land."

The reason that Beira kept Bride captive was her son Angus ever-young, who had fallen in love with Bride after seeing her in a dream. Angus was the antithesis of his mother, warm and gentle where she was cold and harsh. During the winter months he lived apart from her on the Green Isle of the West, also known as the Isle of Youth.

Here we can see the Irish influence on this story. Angus ever-young was clearly derived from Angus MacOg, whose name meant *Angus Young Son*. Bride is a maiden goddess of the Irish pantheon of the Tuatha De Danann. The Green Isle of the West was obviously a reference to Ireland, which is to the west of Scotland and was known as the Emerald Isle. Ireland was also the location of Tir-na-Nog, which means *Land of Youth*.

Angus asked the King of the Green Isle about the maiden in his dreams.

"The King of the Green Isle answered Angus, saying: 'The fair princess whom you saw is Bride, and in the days when you will be King of Summer she will be your queen. Of this your mother, Queen Beira, has full knowledge, and it is her wish to keep you away from Bride, so that her own reign may be prolonged. Tarry here, O Angus, until the flowers been to bloom and the grass begins to grow, and then you shall set free the beautiful Princess Bride.'"

Angus did not want to wait, and decided to rescue Bride, ignoring the advice of the King of the Green Isle, who pointed out that it was the month of the wolf (February), and the temper of wolf weather was always uncertain. So Angus borrowed three days from August and cast a spell on the land and on the sea, causing the Sun to shine and the weather to be fine. Although he searched all across the land on his white horse, Angus could not find Bride. Bride saw Angus in her dreams and wept tears of joy, which formed violets when they touched the ground. Determined to thwart him, Beira raised a gale on the third day which blew Angus back to the Green Isle. Angus returned again and again searching for Bride, until he found her in a forest near Ben Nevis.

> "Said Angus: 'Beautiful princess, I beheld you in a dream weeping tears of sorrow.'
> Bride said: 'Mighty prince, I beheld you in a dream riding over bens and through glens in beauty and power.'
> Said Angus: 'I have come to rescue you from Queen Beira, who has kept you all winter long in captivity.'
> Bride said: 'To me this is a day of great joy.'
> Said Angus: 'It will be a day of great joy to all mankind ever after this.'
> That is why the first day of spring--the day on which Angus found the princess--is called 'Bride's Day'."

Angus and Bride were found by a company of fairy ladies, who took them to the fair court, where they were married with great ceremony. Angus cast magic spells to spread growth across the land. Beira felt Angus' magic and furiously repeatedly struck the ground with her magic wand until it was frozen again. She sent her hag servants out to scour the lands for Angus and Bride, who were driven to the safety of the Green Isle. Angus longed to return to Scotland, and many times crossed the sea, bringing sunshine with him.

"Beira raised storm after storm to drive him away. First she called on the wind named 'The Whistle', which blew high and shrill, and brought down rapid showers of cold hailstones. It lasted for three days, and there was much sorrow and bitterness throughout the length and breadth of Scotland. Sheep and lambs were killed on the moors, and horses and cows perished also.

Angus fled, but he returned soon again. The next wind that Beira raised to prolong her winter reign was the 'Sharp Billed Wind' which is called 'Gobag' lasted for nine days, and all the land was pierced by it, for it pecked and bit in every nook and cranny like a sharp-billed bird.

Angus returned, and the Beira raised the eddy wind which is called 'The Sweeper'. Its whirling gusts tore branches from the budding trees and bright flowers from their stalks. All the time it blew, Beira kept beating the ground with her magic hammer so as to keep the grass from growing. But her efforts were in vain. Spring smiled in beauty all around, and each time she turned away, wearied by her efforts, the sun sprang forth in splendour. The small modest primroses opened their petals in the sunshine, looking forth from cosy nooks that the wind, called 'Sweeper', was unable to reach. Angus fled, but he soon returned again.

Beira was not yet, however, entirely without hope. Her efforts had brought disaster to mankind, and the 'Weeks of Leanness' came on. Food became scarce. The fishermen were unable to venture to sea on account of Beira's tempests, and could get no fish. In the night-time Beira and her hags entered the dwellings of mankind, and stole away their stores of food. It was, indeed, a sorrowful time.

Angus was moved with pity for mankind, and tried to fight the hags of Beira. But the fierce queen raised the "Gales of Complaint" to keep him away, and they raged in fury until the first week of March. Horses and cattle died for want of food, because the fierce winds blew down stacks of fodder and scattered them over the lochs and the ocean. Angus, however, waged a fierce struggle against the hag servants, and at length he drove them away to the north, where they fumed and fretted furiously."

Beira made a final attempt to defeat Angus and maintain winter's dominance. She gathered her hags and smote the clouds with her magic staff, creating the Black Tempest. Winter continued, and Beira borrowed three days from winter to balance the three that Angus had previously borrowed. These three days were tempest spirits riding black hogs, which Beira set free to wreak devastation. For the three days known as the *Hog Days* they froze the land, killing many animals and people with their unexpected bleak cold.

"Beira's reign was now drawing to a close. She found herself unable to combat any longer against the power of the new life that was rising in every vein of the land. The weakness of extreme old age crept upon her, and she longed once again to drink of the waters of the Well of Youth. When, on a bright March morning, she beheld Angus riding over the hills on his white steed, scattering her fierce hag servants before him, she fled away in despair. Ere she went she threw her magic hammer beneath a holly tree, and that is the reason why no grass grows under the holly trees. Beira's black steed went northward with her in flight. As it leapt over Loch Etive it left the marks of

its hoofs on the side of a rocky mountain, and the spot is named to this day 'Horse-shoes'.

She did not rein up her steed until she reached the island of Skye, where she found rest on the summit of the 'Old Wife's Ben' (Ben-e-Caillich) at Broadford. There she sat, gazing steadfastly across the sea, waiting until the day and night would be of equal length. All that equal day she wept tears of sorrow for her lost power, and when night came on she went westward over the sea to Green Island. At the dawn of the day that followed she drank the magic waters of the Well of Youth."

This epic battle between the Cailleach as winter and Angus and Bride as summer, with its different winds and shifting weather patterns, explained the erratic weather patterns of spring. The end of the tale where the Cailleach restored herself with the waters of youth recalls her power over water, and also implies the transformation from crone to maiden found in several of the other Cailleach stories.

3. The Woman of the Mist

Katharine Briggs mentions The Woman of the Mist from local Somerset lore in her *The Fairies in Tradition and Literature*. She is said to be seen in autumn and winter along the hill-top road near Loxey Thorn, and sometimes appears like an old crone gathering sticks.

This description is reminiscent of the Manx Caillagh ny Gyoamagh gathering sticks. She was allegedly seen in the 1920s and 1950s, and those who saw her reported that she appeared to vanish, seemingly becoming part of the mist.

This supernatural disappearance, the stick gathering, the hill-top and the time of her appearances being the dark half of the year all hint at a Cailleach connection. Additionally we may note here the meaning of the name of the Welsh Gwrach-y-Rhybin, who shares some characteristics with the Cailleach, is *hag of the mist.*

CHAPTER 5

OLDEST SPIRIT

An old proverb from West Connacht in Ireland illustrates the great age of the Cailleach in no uncertain terms:

> *"Three great ages; the age of the yew tree, the age of the eagle, and the age of the Cailleach Béarra."*[57]

In fact the great age of the Cailleach is one of the key characteristics she is attributed with in numerous key texts, spanning a period of more than one thousand years. A fragment recorded in the *Carmina Gadelica* emphasised her age through the transformation of the Earth, and her healthy diet, a reference which is also seen in some of the other stories associated with her:

> *"What time the great sea*
> *Was a grey mossy wood,*
> *I was a joyous little maiden,*
> *My wholesome morning meal*
> *The dulse of the Rock of Agir*
> *And the wild garlic of 'Sgoth',*
> *The water of 'Loch-a-Cheann-dubhain',*
> *And the fish of 'Ionnaire-mor',*
> *Those would be my choice sustenance*

---

[57] *The Dolmens of Ireland*, Borlase, 1897

As long as I would live.
I would sow my nine lovely rigs of lint
In the little trim glen of Corradale,
And I would lift my skirtful of nuts
Between the two Torarnises."[58]

It is interesting to note that when she was asked the secret of her age, she recurrently gave an answer associated with the Sidhe (fairy folk). She declared that she never carried the dirt of one place beyond that of another place without washing her feet, thereby not taking the earth from one territory to another. This practice is one commonly associated with fairies, but could also represent a stricture connected with a priesthood.

Likewise, numerous references in regards to the food consumed by the Cailleach occur in stories featuring her and may also represent the memory of a specific strictured diet, found frequently in the practices of formal religious orders.

1. The Cally-Berry

In Ireland there is an interesting farming custom which survived until recent times. The first farmer in a region to finish his harvest would make a corn-dolly, called the Cally-Berry or Cailleach, which was also sometimes known as the Hag of the Harvest. The farmer would then pass this corn-dolly on to the next farmer who finished harvesting, and he would pass it on the next farmer in turn, until it ended up with the last farmer to complete his harvest. This slowest farmer would then be

---

[58] Fragment attributed to Cailleach bheag an f hasaich (*Little Cailleach of the Wild*), *Carmina Gadelica*, Carmichael, 1900.

obliged to look after the Cailleach for the entire winter until the start of the next sowing season.

This was considered very unfortunate in some respects, as the (corn-dolly) Cailleach was said to have a huge appetite, and was thought to eat the farmer who was looking after her, out of house and home. However the farmer could also not dispose of the corn-dolly as doing so was believed to bring him bad luck, as the Cailleach would blight his crops if he slighted her in such a manner.

There was an upside to looking after the Hag of the Harvest though, as the farmer could hang it on his plough-horse for good luck on the first day of ploughing the next spring. So if the farmer could provide hospitality for the Cailleach all winter, he would be rewarded with an extra bountiful harvest the next year.

2. The Cold May-day Monday

After much wandering across the length and breadth of Ireland with her large herd of cows, the Cailleach Bhéarthach eventually settled at Néifinn Mountain. She was considered a very pleasant neighbour with a store of stories that could not be matched. One day a local man who was aware that she was very old asked her if she could tell him about the events of a day hundreds of years earlier. [59] The day was Luan Lae Bhealtaine, the first day of summer, and it had been the coldest day ever.

The Cailleach replied that she had not been there at the time, but the man should go and ask an eagle who lived in the ruins of a particular forge, as he was three

---

[59] IFE 850:526-9.

hundred years older than her and might be able to help. The man sought out the forge of the eagle, who was so old that he had worn the anvil down to the size of a pin with his beak over the centuries. The eagle was unable to help and suggested the man go and ask an even older creature, the Otter of the Rock. When the man found the otter, he also could not help, but suggested the half-blind salmon of Eas Rua as the oldest creature in existence.

The man journeyed to Eas Rua and asked the salmon about the coldest Luan Lae Bhealtaine. The salmon told the man that he remembered the day well, as it was then that he had lost his eye. The salmon explained that he had leaped out of the river to catch a fly, and in the moments he was out in the air the water was turned to ice by the cold. As he lay on the ice a seagull came and pecked one of his eyes out. The salmon's blood melted the ice, rescuing him by from freezing to death by returning him to the unfrozen water at the bottom of the river.

We may note that this story parallels a section of the Irish tale of the *Hawk of Achill* and also the Welsh *Kilhwch and Olwen* tale found in the fourteenth century *White Book of Rhydderch* in both its style and some of the specific details. When Kilhwch and Arthur's knights were searching for the captured Mabon, they went to the Ousel of Cilgwri, who had worn the forge down to a nut with his beak over the centuries. He could not help and sent them to the Stag of Redynvre, who sent them to the Owl of Cwm Cawlwyd. The owl sent them to the Eagle of Gwern Abwy, who sent them to the Salmon of Llyn Llyw. The salmon knew where Mabon was held captive and told the heroes.

The parallels are clear in several details, these being the quest from animal to animal, the forge with the worn-down anvil by centuries of beak rubbing, the eagle being one of the birds, and the salmon of wisdom being the end of the journey.

3. The Cailleach Bhéarthach and the Walker

Legends and stories which were passed down as part of an oral tradition often become embellished, losing some of the finer details along the journey they take through the centuries. Yet they also often preserve knowledge and lore which would otherwise have been lost, this story provides us with one such an example.

It is told that long ago, when the Cailleach Bhéarthach[60] lived at the foot of the Néifinn Mountain in County Mayo, a local man who was renowned for his walking ability went to visit her. He knew she was better than him at walking and wanted to meet her and walk with her. He hoped he might learn something from her about her walking skill, and maybe even gain insights that would make him the best walker in the land.

The man approached the Cailleach and told her he had business in Galway, and wondered whether she might want to buy something in the town and would she walk there with him? The Cailleach agreed as she needed a pair of teasing cards for her wool, and said that she would enjoy the company as it was rare to find anyone who could keep up with her.

The unlikely pair walked to Galway, arriving in very short time, and parted to make their purchases. They

---

60 CBE 159:473-78.

met up again and ate dinner together. After dinner they set off back for home, sometimes running or trotting. Soon they arrived at the foot of the Néifinn, where the river had flooded during the day, preventing them from crossing. Just before they got to the river they had met another man going in the same direction. The Cailleach took the walker who had been accompanying her under her arm and made a running leap, crossing the river.

The other man called across the river asking why the Cailleach hadn't taken him as well. She replied that he had done nothing to her or for her, and that it was not right to come to the aid of every last person, particularly when they didn't need it. In this instance there was a ford nine or ten miles down the river by the waterfall which the man could use to cross the river.

Upon reaching the walker's home the Cailleach asked if his wife had much butter in the house, to which the walker replied that she did have some. The Cailleach instructed him to tell his wife to place a crock of butter with its bottom facing the fire, and its mouth away from the fire, and for him to put his feet on top of the mouth of the butter crock. If he didn't, the Cailleach advised, he would be dead by morning. The man followed her advice and awoke the next morning to find that every last drop of butter had soaked into his feet.

Several points in this story give us insights into the nature of the Cailleach. The first is that the Cailleach takes the walker under her protection, because he went sought her out. She both takes him safely across the river, leaving the other man behind, and provides him with a protection spell on how to use the butter to save his life. This use of butter is clearly as a remedy to enable his body to adjust to the otherworldly encounter he has participated in.

The use of butter, echoes the role of butter and milk as magical substances found in many Celtic and Norse myths.[61] Butter also features in the story of the Cailleach Mhore though she is portrayed in a more negative light.

The Cailleach is described in some tales as milking her deer, and Lady Day or Latha na Caillich (*Cailleach Day*) on 25th March, was particularly associated with milking and charms performed to protect cows, as was Beltane. The survival of milk as an offering to fairy house spirits may also be connected to the early associations of the Cailleach with milk and butter, as well as being a link to her in her role as queen of the fairies.

4. The Cailleach Béarra's Box

The Cailleach Béarra had all sorts of magical abilities, and her wealth was the wealth of the Earth, found in health and wisdom and truth and love, though foolish people often interpreted wealth as gold and coins.

At one point in her ancient history, the Cailleach Béarra lived on the summit of Cnoc na Sidhe (*Hill of the Fairy Mound*), where the wind always blew.[62] When asked, she attributed her good health to her diet, explaining that she ate real, pure madhbhan[63] from Whiddy, duileasg[64] from the harbours of Cape Clear, fish from in the Laune and wild garlic from Bealach Bheimis.

---

[61] See *Milk and the Northern Goddess*, Davidson, 1996, in *The Concept of the Goddess*.
[62] CBE 11:103-5.
[63] An edible seaweed
[64] Dulse

The locals told stories of her great wealth, and the Cailleach knew there were people anxious to ransack her house to steal her perceived fortune. Her prescience revealed that one day a man was going to break into her home, so she went to Sceic in Cuan Leitid and stole a lobster from one of the lobster pots and put it in her money box.

The next day when she was out gathering her food, the thief broke into her house and searched for her money. He found the old box under her bed, and dragged it out. Surprised by its weight he thought it must be full of gold. Then he noticed that there was a hole in the side of the box, which would save him from breaking the top open.

So the lazy thief stuck his hand through the hole into the box and started groping for the money, poking the lobster. The enraged lobster grabbed the thief's hand between its two claws, trapping him, and try as he might the thief could not extricate his hand. The thief was trapped in the Cailleach's lobster trap, and was still caught there when the Cailleach returned home in the evening. The Cailleach took her axe from the wood pile and chopped off the thief's head, in a clear warning that it doesn't pay to steal from wise old women.

5. Never Ask A Woman Her Age

One day a friar and his companion boy were travelling and found themselves at the house of the Cailleach Bhéarthach.[65] The friar greeted her, saying *"God save you"*, to which the Cailleach replied *"the same*

---

[65] Recorded in *An Sgeulaidhe Gaedhealach*, De hÍde, 1933.

man save yourself". The Cailleach invited the friar and his companion into the house, for it was cold outside. After warming himself by the fire, the friar asked the Cailleach her age, knowing that she was very old. The Cailleach replied that every year since she came of age (i.e. eighteen), she had killed a cow and thrown its bones into the loft, so all they needed to do was count the bones in the loft to determine her exact age.

The friar sent his boy up into the loft, and the boy called down that it was full of bones and he would need to throw them down to count them. The friar sat and kept count until he was very tired, and then asked the boy if they were nearing the end. The boy replied that they had not even cleared one corner of the loft yet, so the friar told him to come down and throw all the bones back into the loft.

The friar acknowledged the great age of the Cailleach and commented that in all the many years she must have seen many marvellous sights. He politely asked her what the most marvellous thing she had seen in all her years was, to which the Cailleach responded by recalling a tale from her youth. She spoke of how she had been milking the cows one fine day with another girl when she saw a great blackness in the sky. Thinking it was about to storm she hurried the girl on with the milking.

Then the Cailleach saw a woman in white rush past her in the air, overtaking the wind. Shortly afterwards came two large mastiffs, with huge tongues and fire bellowing out of their mouths. This was followed by a flaming black coach with the Devil inside. The Cailleach asked the Devil why he was chasing the woman, and the Devil explained that she had brought scandal upon a priest and died in a state of deadly sin, and if he caught her before she got to the gates of heaven he would gain her soul, but if she made it to the gates of heaven the Virgin Mary would intercede for her and have her taken into heaven.

After hearing this tale, the friar asked if the Cailleach had seen any other marvels in all her years. The Cailleach told another tale, regarding the funeral of a friend of hers.

When she arrived at the funeral nobody could lift the coffin up. Twelve men tried to carry the coffin and could not even lift it; it seemed to be heavier than solid stone. When the Cailleach asked what her dead friend's profession had been, she was told he had been a herder. Following this four unknown men arrived who said they were herders, who lifted the coffin to their shoulders with such ease that it seemed to be empty.

The mysterious men then started walking, leading the funeral procession. They walked through the night, up and down hills, leaving people behind, with some fainting or dying of exhaustion. Then in a dark wood the ground opened up and swallowed all those who were still following the four men with the coffin. Trapped within the Earth, the Cailleach prayed. After four days of prayer a tiny hole opened up, and after another three (making an entire week of prayer) the hole was large enough to climb out. She emerged from the hole and spent five weeks travelling the route back to the location of the original funeral ceremony, even though it only took an afternoon of processing after the coffin for her to travel away from it.

After telling these tales to the friar, the Cailleach remarked that it was no wonder that she was grey and withered with her life having been through such perils, and the friar replied that she was a fine hardy old woman.

In another version of this tale of the Friar is replaced by Saint Patrick, who was too impatient to count the bones which revealed her age and instead made her disappear in a red flash of misogynistic divine Christian power.[66]

---

[66] CBE 74:261-62.

CHAPTER 6

LADY OF THE BEASTS

Although she was known to protect all types of animals, the deer were most beloved of the Cailleach in Scotland. Stories tell of how she treated them as her cattle, herding and milking them and protecting them from hunters. The Cailleach Mhor Nam Fiadh (*Great Cailleach of the Deer*) was known to kill any man not from the island of Jura who set foot on the island with a view to hunting and killing her deer. This fits with the description given by Ross in her classic work *Pagan Celtic Britain* when she declared that the Cailleachan survived in local folklore as *"great supernatural hags haunting mountain passes or driving their deer over the hills and conferring benefits and evils on humanity as they saw fit."*

The Cailleach Beinn Na Bric (*Cailleach of Speckled Mountain*) was known to the local hunters and advised them on the condition of the deer, how many they could hunt and when. The hunters always respected her advice, knowing that she guarded the animals and controlled the balance of nature. She was believed to have unlimited power over the elements and could charm animals with her magic songs.[67]

---

[67] *Cailleach Beinn Na Bric*, S.M.R., 1823.

Thus a local story from the Grampians tells of how the Cailleach told two boys where to find a particular deer, but they ignored her advice and caught a stag instead. When they returned home, they discovered they had an empty rope and no stag.

This is clearly reminiscent of the idea we have suggested of a priesthood associated with the Cailleach, an idea which was postulated by J G Mackay in 1932 with regard to a deer cult. Writing in the magazine *Folklore* he suggested:

> "The deer-priestesses never appear in the tales as priestesses, but as witches. They gave the hunters blessings and charms to procure them success in the chase, and afterwards shared the spoils of the chase with them. After all witches are only fossil priestesses, the exponents of dead pagan faiths."[68]

Mackenzie also continued this line of thought, suggesting in his work *Scottish Folk-Lore and Folk Life* (1935) that,

> "The gigantic stature of these Old Women, their love for their deer, the fact that their dealings are almost exclusively with hunters, and the fact that each is referred to as a bean-sidhe, or supernatural woman, seems sufficient warrant for calling them Deer-Goddesses ...They are all creatures of the wild. This is very significant, and suggests a very great antiquity."[69]

However as previously mentioned she not only protected the deer, and she was also known to protect

---

[68] *The Deer-Cult & the Deer-Goddess Gult of the Ancient Caledonians*, Mackay, 1932.
[69] *Scottish Folk Lore and Folk Life*, Mackenzie, 1935.

wild pigs and boars, wild goats, wild cattle and wolves. It is interesting to note that all of these animals may be found in herds and packs.

The Cailleach had a strong connection with the bird kingdom, particularly herons, which she shape-shifted into in several tales. The connection to the heron provided a link to the Celtic sea god Manannan, who is found in two of the Cailleach stories, and was sometimes considered to be her husband. We may also note that the Scottish Gaelic name for a barn owl is *Cailleach-oidhche gheal*, or *white night hag*.

In some texts like the twelfth century *Metrical Dindshenchas* the Cailleach was mentioned as being one of the two wives of the god Lugh, with her personal name being Bui or Boi (*yellow*). Significantly, it has been suggested by Professor Wagner that the word Bui/Boi comes from the Indo-European form *Buvyā meaning *white cow-like one*, the same root that forms the goddess name Boand, the white cow goddess. This would then suggest a possible connection between the Cailleach Béarra, who is a cattle goddess and Boann, who is a cow goddess. Cows occur as the sacred animal of the Cailleach in Irish tales in the same way that deer do in the Scottish ones.

The cattle connection occurred in the story of *The Expulsion of the Dessi*, where the Cailleach is found under her name of Boi. She played a role with her red-eared white cow (i.e. fairy cow) in the upbringing of the boy Corc, who was the product of incest. After a year the cow leaped into the sea and turned into a stone, which was called Bo Boi, and the island nearby was called Inis Boi (*the Island of Boi*).

The Cailleach was often said to keep cows, and indeed her cows were described as being fairy cows, which gave great amounts of milk. At Acha-na m-ba (*Field of the Cows*) in Benderloch in the West Highlands the circular green hollows are known as *the Cailleach Bheur's cheese vats*. According to Mackenzie there was a rock shelter in Ardnamurchan called the Caillich's Byre, where she said to keep her cattle.

There is an interesting reference in Maclagan's *Religio Scotica* to the Cailleach restoring the dead, with an implied magical use of milk.

> *"The re-vivifying the dead is also generally ascribed to a Cailleach with what by F. W. Campbell is called "hallan iochslaint ...the teat of the healing balsam"*[70]

This is reminiscent of the Morrígan in the Irish epic *Táin Bó Cúailnge*, who heals her own wounds by feeding magical healing milk to the hero Cú Chulainn, tricking him into giving his blessings which heal the wounds he inflicted.

> *"There came the Morrígan, daughter of Ernmas, from the side in the guise of an old woman and in Cú Chulainn's presence she milked a cow with three teats."*[71]

1. The Lucky Poachers

In his book *The Art of Deer-Stalking*, William Scrope recounted a tale of two poachers from 1773. The story

---

[70] *Religio Scotica*, Maclagan, 1909.
[71] *Táin Bó Cúailnge,* C12 CE.

emphasises the supernatural nature of the Cailleach and her role as Lady of the Beasts, though it could also hint at the figure of a priestess of the Cailleach guarding the deer, as suggested by Mackay.

The two poachers set out in search of red deer. They headed towards the forest of Atholl and were caught in a snowstorm from the north. The storm soon cleared and they located some deer, shooting and wounding a hind. They trailed the hind through the trail of her blood in the snow, until the snow returned, much stronger. They sheltered under their plaids in the lee of some rocks, eating their oatcakes and drinking their whisky, and slept through the night.

In the morning the snow was still blowing hard, reducing visibility to a few metres. They struggled out, keeping the north wind to their backs and trying to head for home. However the wind veered to the east, and with no visible landmarks, the poachers did not realise and carried on with the wind at their backs, heading west rather than south.

With their provisions running out and the prospect of another night in the rocks, the men were delighted when they saw an old sheiling bothy ahead. This was a traditional summer dwelling for men and women who looked after the cattle in summer when they were ni the high pastures, and so it was unlikely to be used in winter.

As the men approached, the door opened and a wild and haggard old woman opened the door and beckoned them in. She told them she had been expecting them, and their supper and beds were ready for them. Startled the men followed her in to the bothy and sat down at the table where two plates were ready with oat cakes and bannocks. As the woman poured soup from the pot where it bubbled, she crooned a song in an unfamiliar language. The men realised magic was afoot and were reluctant to eat. As they sat terrified, the old woman held up a rope with three knots in it and told them of her power over the weather.

> "If I lowse the first [knot], there shall blaw a fair wind, such as the deer stalker may wish; if I lowse the second, a stronger blast shall sweep o'er the hills; and if I lowse the third, sic a storm will brak out, as neither man nor beast can thole; and the blast shall yowl down the corries and the glens, and the pines shall faw crashin into the torrents, and this bare arm shall guide the course o the storm, as I sit on my throne of Cairn-Gower, on the tap o Ben-y-Gloe. Weel did ye ken my pouer the day, when the wind was cauld and dedly, and all was dimmed in snaw - and ye see that ye was expectit here, and ye hae brought nae venison; but if ye mean to thrive, ye maun place a fat hart, or a yeld [barren] hind in the braes o' Atholl, by Fraser's cairn, at midnight, the first Monday in every month, while the season lasts. If ye neglect this my biddin, foul will befaw ye, and the fate of Walter o Rhuairm shall owertak ye; ye shall surely perish in the waste; the raven shall croak yer dirge; and yer bones shall be pickit by the eagle."[72]

The poachers gave their word to do as the old woman asked, ate her food and fell asleep. When they woke late in the morning the bothy was deserted and there was no sign of the old woman. The storm had ceased and the men were able to find their way home.

---

[72] Scrope, William; *The Art of Deer-Stalking*; 1839; John Murray; London

Scrope goes on to refer to the woman as the Witch of Ben-y-gloe, saying this was the last time she was seen by mortal men. We may note here that the selling of knotted strings or ropes to sailors was a popular practice amongst witches for many centuries. The chanting in an unknown language and the insistence on a regular offering of a deer would fit with a priestess or witch cunningly ensuring her food supplies were provided.

2. The Cailleach and the Stupid Deer

The squire to Lord Reay in Sutherland was a young man called William. One day the squire got lost in the wood, and found himself in a grove he had never seen before. Nestled in the grove was a hut, almost undetectable except for its windows peering out of the undergrowth like eyes. William was intrigued and entered the hut to try and get a clue as to the identity of the mysterious occupant of the hidden house. As he entered the hut he noticed blue yarn hanging off a nail by the door.

Inside the hut William quickly realised that the hut belonged to a carlin (witch). He saw bunches of herbs hung from the rafters, and a cauldron sat in the corner. As he looked around, he heard a noise outside and hid in the pantry, peering out of a crack in the door. William saw the door open, and the figure of the Cailleach stood on the threshold. Behind her a whole herd of deer milled like grazing sheep.

William was astonished by the way the deer gazed at her adoringly, and he noticed that one of the deer was eating the blue yarn hanging by the door. The Cailleach struck the deer with her staff, saying *"The spell is off you; and Lord Reay's bullet will be your death today."*

After an uncomfortable night hardly daring to move or breathe in the Cailleach's pantry for fear of her power, William was relieved when she left in the morning. Hurrying through the woods he managed to find familiar landmarks and made his way back to his master, who was about to set out on a hunt. Lord Reay laughed at the tale told by his gullible squire, but the joke was on him, for later in the day he shot a fine yellow hind, and in its stomach was found a hank of blue yarn.

3. The Cailleach's Song

In an account recorded in 1823, the Cailleach Beinn Na Bric was described as protectress of the deer, and a translation of the Gaelic song she sang as she scared a hunter away was given. How a terrified hunter managed to remember the whole song is not mentioned, but the song is descriptive of a number of the attributes of the Cailleach:

> *"Tiny hunter cease to roam*
> *O'er the piny heights where I make my dwelling;*
> *Tempt the roaring foam*
> *Of ocean, when high the trouble waves are swelling;*
> *But here, where I hold my sway,*
> *O'er deep glen, and mountain gray,*
> *Dare not venture night or day –*
> *Tiny mortal roam not here!*
> *I am monarch of the deer,*
> *Which bound over all these green mountains;*
> *I partake of their cheer,*
> *The crystal stream so clear,*
> *And the cresses that fringe the blue fountains:*

'Tis I that deface heaven's face with the storm,
And sublime on the dark clouds career.

I revel mid the elemental war,
At rest within my misty car,
And send my voice, in hollow moans, afar,
Down the dusky glen, among the dwellings of men;
And fill them with terror and fear!

Tremble mortal, at my power,
Leave my sacred dominion!
Ere I cause the heavens lower,
And whelm thee with a fearful shower,
For sport to my fairy minions!

Hence away, child of clay,
Go, tempt the roaring foam
Of ocean, when high the troubled waves are
swelling;
But ne'er again stray where I hold my sway,
O'er the piny heights that I make my dwelling!"[73]

4. The Story of Mongan

The Cailleach is not the main character in this classic Irish tale, however her role is significant in laying the foundations for the events that follow. It is also interesting to note that the beneficiary of the events is the sea god Manannan MacLir, who is described elsewhere as the husband of the Cailleach Béarra. The whole story would be too long to recount here, but the parts pertaining to the Cailleach are significant in showing her connection with cattle again, in this instance otherworldly cattle, as white skinned and red-eared animals always are in Celtic myths.

---

[73] *Cailleach Beinn Na Bric*, S.M.R., 1823.

One day Fiachna the Blonde (one of the descendants of King Niall) went to visit the King of Lochlann (*Scandinavia*). The king was sick, and his advisors and magicians informed Fiachna that he could only be healed by eating the flesh of a white-skinned cow with red ears. The only cow of this kind belonged to the Cailleach Dubh (*black Cailleach*). Fiachna, as a good guest, undertook the healing of the king, and went to visit the Cailleach Dubh.

She agreed to give him the cow, but only if he would give his guarantee and also four other cows to replace it. Fiachna agreed and took the cow to the king, only to be informed by a messenger who caught up with him that he has been chosen in his absence to become the king of Ulster. Fiachna immediately returned to his realm to take up his new role as sovereign and all was well for a year.

Then one day Fiachna heard cries coming from in front of his fortress and sent his men to investigate. His men returned with the Cailleach Dubh, who complained that she had been tricked by the King of Lochlann, and as her guarantor he had to gain compensation for her. Fiachna offered the Cailleach more cows, but she refused, instead demanding that Fiachna go and make war on the King of Lochlann.

Fiachan took his troops and attacked Lochlann. For the first three days the fight was turning against Fiachna's men. Though Fiachna himself killed three hundred warriors, the King of Lochlann released a monstrous ram that killed three hundred of Fiachna's men in return. Fiachna vowed to go and fight the ram, but his men persuaded him against this course of action.

As they counselled him a huge warrior arrived and offered to help. Fiachna agreed and offered the warrior whatever he wanted for his help. The warrior, who was Manannan MacLir in disguise, agreed and released an enormous dog from under his cloak which killed the ram.

Manannan then went to Ireland in the guise of Fiachna and slept with Fiachna's wife, making her pregnant with a son, who would be a hero in his own right. Fiachna subsequently compensated the Cailleach with seven fortresses and a hundred cattle. The tale continued, describing the saga of Fiachna, but the Cailleach played no further role in it

5. The Old Woman Outwits the Devil

The heroine of this tale is commonly recorded as an old woman rather than the Cailleach, but the motifs found throughout it clearly show parallels to those associated with the Cailleach. In our opinion the combination of the old woman (which is the meaning of the name Cailleach), cow, flooded river, and broken apron of stones provides too many coincidental similarities to be ignored.

Our story begins with the Devil crossing North Yorkshire when a high wind tore his apron strings and he dropped all the stones he was carrying in it. The collection of stones was subsequently known as the Devil's Apron Strings, or the Apron Full of Stones, which is still visible near Carnforth today.

That is only the beginning of the story. The Old Woman was looking for one of her cows which had strayed over the river Lune, but the river had flooded and she could not cross it. At this point the Devil appeared to her, offering to build her a bridge by the next morning. This he would do on one condition, which was that the first living soul to cross the completed bridge would be his. The Old Woman agreed to this and the Devil got to work. When he ran out of stones, he reclaimed some of those he had left at the Apron Full of Stones in order to complete the bridge.

At dawn the bridge was ready and the Devil waited keenly for the Old Woman to cross the bridge. She walked across the bridge by herself, and the Devil could barely contain his pleasure at the thought of gaining such an ancient soul. But, the Old Woman was not going to let herself be caught, she took a bun out of her bag and threw it across the bridge. A tiny dog leaped from inside her shawl to the other side of the bridge in pursuit of the bun, becoming the first living soul to cross it. At this the Devil left in disgust, realising that he had been outwitted by the Old Woman. He was so angry that he did not even bother taking the soul of the Old Woman's canine friend.

6. The Cailleach Ends the Viking Age

The Cailleach was sometimes described as riding astride a giant white wolf which is an interesting connection in light of a description given by Branston regarding the failed invasion attempt by Harold Hardrada in 1066 in *The Lost Gods of England*:

> "It is written that before the Norman invasion of England, Gyrth had a dream that a great witch stood on the island, opposing the king's fleet with a fork and a trough. Tord dreamed that "before the army of the people of the country was a riding a huge witch-wife upon a wolf," and she tossed the invading soldiers into its mouth."

This is reminiscent of the Cailleach, especially when we take into consideration some of her other roles, in particular that of bestower of sovereignty. That the witch-wife in this story is seen defending the north of England, where the Cailleach was strongest in England, is also highly suggestive and appropriate. The defeat of Harold Hardrada's forces by those of Harold Godwinson at the Battle of Stamford Bridge in 1066 is now sometimes described as the end of the Viking age.

7. The mark left by Cailleach Béarra

Have you ever wondered, why does it take so long for the young of the human race to learn to walk, whilst it seems to come as a natural thing for the offspring of other species? One explanation given for this was the influence of the Cailleach Béarra. [74] It was said that in the distant past, in the time before time was measured in calendars, she put her hand in the small of a baby's back when it was born, causing all human children to come into the world unable to walk.

This is a strange piece of folklore, recorded in the middle of the twentieth century and seems to perpetuate the negative image of the Cailleach. Alternatively, in a symbolic form this could be seen as the Cailleach forming humanity in the same way as she formed the landscape.

----

[74] CBE 788:130-31.

Chapter 7

SHAPESHIFTER

In many of the Cailleach tales the motif of transformation from crone to maiden, symbolizing the shifting seasons of the year, and also tying in to the bestowal of sovereignty, can clearly be found. This is also seen in the well-known tale of Thomas the Rhymer, where the Fairy Queen may well be a survival of the Cailleach into popular lore and literature. The idea of an old woman transforming into a young maiden could also be given a mundane explanation if we give credence to the idea of a priestess cult, in which the older priestesses took responsibility for the younger generation, gradually allowing them to take on some of the responsibility, until such time they could take over.

Many of the Cailleach tales have the motif of transformation from crone to maiden, symbolizing the shifting seasons of the year, and also tying in to the bestowal of sovereignty. This is also seen in the well-known tale of Thomas the Rhymer, where the Fairy Queen may well be a survival of the Cailleach into popular lore and literature. As previously mentioned, the idea of an old woman transforming into a maiden could easily be explained by experienced older priestesses and neophytes at the beginning of their training swapping places.

The Scottish tale of the Cailleach Bheur and Loch Bà illustrates the transformative theme found in some of the winter goddess tales, but on a much longer timescale. There are different versions of this tale, of which we have chosen two to illustrate its themes.

The examples of the Cailleach shapeshifting into an animal have interesting connotations, like the Caillagh ny Gyoamagh and the Cailleach both shifting into heron form, and the Gyre Carling shifting into a sow. The wearing of animal and bird skins by priesthoods around the world is well documented through the ages, and the animal shapeshifting motif in the Cailleach stories may also have such origins.

The transformation into stone at the beginning of summer seen in some of the tales symbolises a seasonal shift, the hard cold stone representing the bleakness of winter being contained through the warmer months, to be released again when winter returns. The stone may also recall the frequent tales of her carrying stones.

1. The Cailleach Bheur and Loch Bà (I)

The Cailleach Bheur had dwelt on the headland of Mull from before time immemorial. The Cailleach Bheur was said to be a young girl when Adam and Eve were still enjoying the Garden of Eden. When asked her age she said of herself,

> *"When the ocean was a forest with its firewood, I was then a young lass."*[75]

[75] University of Edinburgh MSS AM/35.8 Mull.

The Cailleach Bheur had evaded death by transforming herself through a hundred year cycle. Two years prior to the end of the century she would dramatically age in appearance, she would go pale, her hair gray and her back would stoop. It was however not a problem for her, as she could shift back into the form of a beautiful young maiden by bathing herself in the waters of Loch Bà. She would completely immerse herself in the waters during the liminal dawn moment, prior to any other living creature greeting the sunrise in order to ensure her transformation.

On one such occasion, the Cailleach was descending to the shore of Loch Bà as the sun rose in the east. As she prepared to step into the water she heard a dog barking in the distance. The noise of the barking echoed off the cliffs around Loch Bà and she fell to the ground and died. The dog had greeted the Sun before she could undergo her transformation. As she died she called out:

> "It's early the dog spoke,
> in advance of me,
> The dog, in advance of me;
> the dog, in advance of me.
> It's early the dog spoke,
> in advance of me,
> In the quiet of the morning,
> across Loch Bà."

2. The Cailleach Bheur and Loch Bà (II)

In a second version of this tale the Cailleach's gigantic size is emphasised.[76] This version described her as being huge and having a single eye in the centre of her forehead, with a herd of three cows. The cows are

---

[76] University of Edinburgh MSS SA 1953/49/B5.

interesting as she is more commonly associated with deer in Scotland, cows being an Irish motif. In the tale her size is set against the context of the lakes in the landscape.

> *"Dark, deep Crùlachan*
> *The deepest loch in the world*
> *The Straits of Mull used to reach as far as my knees*
> *But Crùlachan used to reach to my thighs."*

The other major differences to the tale are that the Cailleach recounted more memories of how the world was when she was young, a version of the flooding well tale, where she forgot to cover her well with its stone lid and had to quickly cover it. The result was the creation of Loch Obha. The other difference is that the dog which barked belonged to a shepherd who knew of her transformation but had forgotten to tie his dog up.

3. Thomas the Rhymer

Thomas the Rhymer, or True Tom, has been immortalized in verse for centuries as the lover of the Fairy Queen. He seems to have been based on the historical figure of Thomas of Erceldoune, who was born in the early thirteenth century. The Fairy Queen is an interesting figure as the earliest version of the tale described her transformation from beautiful maiden to blue-skinned hag, (*"bloo as beten led"* – blue as beaten lead) in the same manner as the Cailleach's transformation from winter queen to summer maiden. This then suggests that the Cailleach tales may have been a possible origin for this tale.

"Thomas stondand in that sted
And beheld that lady gay
hir here that hong vpon hir hed,
her een semyd out, that were so gray.
And alle hir [rich] clothis were Away.
that there before saw in that stede;
the toothe blak, the tothur gray,
the body bloo as beten led."[77]

The Fairy Queen bestowed the power of prophecy on Thomas, or in a different version gave him a cursed fruit which prevented him from lying. She also made prophecies concerning the outcome of battles and claims to Sovereignty, both of which are Cailleach characteristics. These include the battle of Falkirk in 1298, the battle of Halidon Hill in 1333, the battle of Otterbourn in 1387, and Henry IV's invasion of Scotland in 1401.

---

[77] Cambridge University MS, p119.

CHAPTER 8

BESTOWER OF SOVEREIGNTY

The Cailleach has frequently been considered to be an ancient Earth goddess, whilst also taking the role of liminal crone, and it is not difficult to see why she should be seen in the role of bestower of sovereignty. This role has been recognized for some time, as seen in *The Book of the Cailleach* (2003) where Gearoid O Crualaoich observed, *"Cailleach Béarra, the hag/mother goddess of Beara is also known at the learned, literary level as a personification of the territorial sovereignty queen."* This comment is reinforced by similar declarations based on the tales in other academic works such as *The Oxford Companion to Irish Literature* (1996).

The tale of Princess Beara is interesting in this light, as not only does it make the link between Spain and Ireland suggested earlier in the migration of the Celtiberians, but it also has a sovereignty aspect attached to a human figure. The princess not only married Eoghan, but also provided an army to enable him to return from exile and reclaim his land. Thus she effectively bestowed the sovereignty of his land back on him, albeit by force of arms.

Several myths have an unnamed crone goddess bestowing sovereignty onto the worthy candidate, and transforming into a beautiful maiden as she does so, in a similar manner to the Cailleach's transformation in some of the stories about her. Whilst these tales may not specifically refer to the Cailleach by name, the absence of name and coincidence of roles and motifs does suggest that they could be about her.

This theme of the hag/maiden Bestower of Sovereignty was common in popular literature throughout Britain during the fourteenth and fifteenth century, probably as a survival of earlier myths. As well as the tales discussed the theme of the transformed crone also occured in *The Wedding of Sir Gawain and Dame Ragnell*, *The Marriage of Sir Gawain*, *The Tale of Florent*, *The Ballad of King Henry*, *The Ballad of Kemp Owyne* and *The Ballad of the Knight and the Shepherd's Daughter*. Chaucer also covered this theme in *The Wife of Bath's Tale*.[78]

1. Princess Beara

The King of Spain was very proud of his extremely beautiful daughter, princess Beara. One day the king summoned his druid, to ask him when his daughter would get married, and to who. The druid informed the king that his future son-in-law would arrive in Spain that very night. From his visions, he gave the king instructions to deliver to Beara in order to locate her spouse. She was to go eastward to the river Eibhear, where she would find a crimson-spotted salmon dressed

---

[78] *The Wife of Bath's Tale*, Chaucer (1342-1400).

from head to tail in shining golden clothing. Beara had to strip the clothing off the salmon and make a shirt for her future spouse out of it. Beara followed the instructions her father gave her, going to the river and finding the salmon just as the druid had predicted. She stripped the salmon of his golden clothing and made a shirt out of it as instructed.

That night the exiled king Eoghan arrived at the king's court, having been driven out of Ireland. Despite their attraction Eoghan did not ask for Beara's hand. The king's druid asked Eoghan why he did not court Beara, to which Eoghan replied it would not be fitting for an exile to make such assumptions. He added that the princess Beara was dear to him and he was grateful for the friendship of the king. When the king heard Eoghan's answer he declared it was the answer of a king, exiled or not. He told Beara to sit on Eoghan's right hand at the feast that night and present him with the shirt she had made. When Eoghan put the shirt on over his armour it glistened in all directions, resulting in him being named Eoghan the Bright.

Eoghan returned to Ireland with his new wife Beara and a Spanish army to reclaim his territory. They landed on the peninsula which he named after her, and which has borne her name ever since, the Beara peninsula.

2. Niall of the Nine Hostages

The Irish eleventh century tale of *Niall of the Nine Hostages* placed the sovereign bestowing crone at the centre of the story.[79]   Niall and his four older brothers became lost in a wood and were all desperately thirsty. They came upon a crone (possibly the Cailleach) guarding a well and asked her for a drink of water from her well. The crone responded by demanding a kiss from anyone who wished to drink from the well. Niall's four brothers all refused the crone's offer (we can see here the magical connotations of water and the well as symbolising the magic of the Otherworld and the entrance to the transformatory womb of the Earth). Niall however did not reject the crone, but rather accepted the *"hideous shape, thin-shanked, grey-headed, bushy-browed"* figure.   He even went so far as to *"around her he closed his arms … he strained her to his breast and bosom, as though she were for ever his own spouse."*[80]

During the embrace the crone transformed herself into the most beautiful maiden imaginable, described in the story as *"the fairest in human form"*.   Niall asked the woman her name and was told, *"I am Sovereignty"*.[81]   She then went on to make a prophecy, and compared his reign allegorically to their embrace, with a rough beginning, smooth middle and peaceful end.

3. The Adventure of Daire's Sons

The *Adventure of Daire's Sons* also contains the motif of the crone (possibly Cailleach) who is sovereignty in disguise.   Five brothers, all called Lughaid, were out hunting when they were caught in a snowstorm.

---

[79] From *Echtra Mac Echach Muigmeddóin* (*The Adventure of the Sons of Eochaid Muigmedón*).
[80] *Echtra Mac Echach Muigmeddóin.*
[81] *Echtra Mac Echach Muigmeddóin.*

Desperately seeking shelter, they found a hut owned by a crone, who demanded that they sleep with her in exchange for shelter. All of the brothers refused to countenance the idea and turned her down except for the youngest of them, Lughaid Láigde. By sleeping with the crone who transformed into the beautiful maiden, Lughaid Láigde gained the sovereignty of Ireland.

> *"The hag entered the bed, and Lughaid followed her. It seemed to him that the radiance of her face was the sun rising in the month of May. A purple bordered gown she wore, and she had beautifully coloured hair. Her fragrance was likened to a fragrant herb-garden. Then he mingled in love with her. "Auspicious is thy journey," said she, "I am Sovereignty, and the kingship of Erin will be obtained by thee.""*[82]

4. The Daughter of the King under the Waves

This motif also occurred in Scottish as well as Irish tales, as can be seen from the West Highlands story *Nighean Righ fo Thuinn* (*The Daughter of the King under the Waves*).[83] One stormy night the Feen brothers were disturbed by a knock on the door of their cottage. When they answered the door they saw a loathsome hag (again possibly the Cailleach), who begged a place inside out of the rain to warm herself by the fire.

The two older brothers, Fionn and Oisin refused to admit the hag into their cottage, but the youngest brother Diarmaid, pleaded with his two elder siblings that she should be allowed in to warm herself. During the night

---

[82] *Cóir Anmanni* (*Fitness of Names*).
[83] *Popular Tales of the West Highlands* (Volume 3), Campbell, 1860.

the hag crept into Diarmaid's bed, which he responded to by placing a fold of blanket between them. After a while however he discovered to his amazement that she had changed into the most beautiful woman he had ever seen.

CHAPTER 9

SEER & FORETELLER OF DOOM

The ability to tell the future has been associated both with deities and with priestesses and witches. Pythonesses and sibyls were significant figures in the ancient world, uttering the words of the gods (and goddesses) when in trance. If the Cailleach stories do represent the survival of an ancient priestess cult, it would make sense that the ability to foresee the future would be one of the associated abilities.

The Cailleach only displayed her ability to predict the future in a small number of tales. In all the stories the Cailleach never told lies, although she may have only told part of the truth, and sometimes she was very cryptic, in the manner of an oracle.

On occasions she clearly seemed to demonstrate trickster qualities. This humour and subtlety often seems to be lost in modern interpretations of the Cailleach, a fact which should be obvious to anyone who appreciates their elderly female relatives and friends!

1. The Caillagh ny Gueshag

The Manx figure of the Caillagh ny Gueshag (*Cailleach of the spells*) has survived as in local lore as a prophetess. This again suggests a possible root with a real person, whose sayings stood out enough to be recorded. She made some curious predictions, like:

> *"There shall be a smithy chimney in every house before the end of the world."*

> *"Out of grey stones people will get their bread."*

However a more striking prediction was the one that a time would come when the Manx would be able to travel without wetting their feet from the point of Ayre to Scotland, a twenty mile or so journey, which is shrinking and may yet come to pass as more extreme weather changes cause the distance to shorten.[84]

2. The Golden Apples of Lough-Erne

In this story the Cailleach displayed cunning in her demand of reward and there is also a sense of her knowing the queen will undo herself in her eagerness. The rewards demanded by the Cailleach hint at a clever woman setting herself up for life at the expense of the malicious queen.

Conn-eda was the beloved son of the king of the western districts of Ireland, hated by his stepmother, who wanted her son to have the succession that would pass to

---

[84] *Mona Miscellany: A Selection of Proverbs, Sayings, Ballads, Customs, Superstitions, & Legends, Peculiar to the Isle of Man,* Harrison, 1873.

Conn-eda. His stepmother tried to damage his reputation by spreading gossip about him, but Conn-eda was so beloved of his people that nobody would believe it. Eventually his stepmother decided to visit the Cailleach of Lough Carrib to gain her advice.

Early one morning she went to the Cailleach's cabin and told her the story as she saw it. However, the canny Cailleach told her that she could not help until she received her reward. The queen impatiently demanded to know what reward she required, and the Cailleach replied that she would have to have the cavity of her arm filled with wool, and the hole she bored with her distaff filled with red wheat.

The queen agreed, whereupon the Cailleach stood in the door of her hut and bent her arm to make a circle at her side, and directed the queen's attendants to thrust the wool through her arm. This continued until the whole house was filled with wool. The Cailleach then took the queen and her attendants to her brother's house and climbed on the roof, making a hole in it with her distaff. The attendants poured red wheat through the whole in the roof until the whole house was completely filled and not another grain could fit in.

Once she had received her reward, the Cailleach handed a chess board and set of pieces to the Queen. She told her to invite the prince to play with her and she would win the first game. Likewise she should impose the condition that whoever won a game could impose geasa (conditions or strictures) on the loser. Then she should bid the prince to either go into exile or procure the three golden apples, black steed and magical hound from the king of the Fir Bolgs within a year and a day.

The queen went to the prince and invited him to play chess. As the Cailleach had predicted she won the first game easily, but in her eagerness she challenged him to a second game which she lost. After the queen had imposed her geasa,[85] the prince imposed his geis that she had to sit on the pinnacle of a certain tower taking no food except whatever red wheat she could pick up with the point of her bodkin until his return or the year and the day expired. As is usually the case, the prince managed to acquire the items with some supernatural aid, and the frustrated queen killed herself by jumping from the tower on his return.

3. Foreteller of Doom

The old woman foreteller of doom associated with water was a figure found throughout the Celtic world. Some of these figures have a lot in common with the Cailleach, and may be derived from her. For this reason we have included reference to figures that have a number of motifs in common with her, though they may have disparate roots and not necessarily be connected. Nevertheless the parallels are interesting and worthy of note.

A description of the Washer at the Ford figure as a hag who sounds very like the Cailleach appears in the late fifteenth century text *Caithréimm Thoirdhealbhaigh*.[86] The descriptions from the story refer to battles fought in 1317/8 and she is called the Brónach Bóirne (*brónach of*

---

[85] Geis (singular) or geasa (plural) refers to binding strictures/taboos which the recipient must obey.
[86] *Caithréimm Thoirdhealbhaigh* (*The Triumphs of Turlough*), Magrath, 1495.

Ceann Bóirne) or *Hag of the Black Head,* referring to a peninsula in northwest Clare. The description is very similar to some of those of the Scottish Cailleach Bheur:

> *"Over the shore of the bright lake rose a long great, stooped, blue-faced, wretched, hunchbacked, grey-toothed, coarse-furred, crook-nailed, tall, lean, red hag. The appearance of that spectral, squinting, watery-eyed, crooked, bent-shanked creature was like this: she had shaggy, rough-stranded, garlanded hair rough as heather, red and grey, which resembled seaweed."*[87]

The Gwrach-y-Rhybin (*hag of the mist*) was a hideous fairy hag who lived in Wales and haunted certain old aristocratic Welsh families. She was also said to haunt Pennard Castle and the banks of the river Dribble. The Gwrach-y-Rhybin was described as being winged, with matted black hair, overlong arms, black teeth and a hooked nose. She was said to flap her wings against the window at night and howl the name of the person who will die.[88]

She also had another form, when she was called the yr Hen Chrwchwd (*old hump-backed one*), in which she appeared as a shrieking old woman, whose cries presaged the death of a local person.[89]

---

[87] *Caithréimm Thoirdhealbhaigh.*
[88] *British Goblins: Welsh Folklore, Fairy Mythology, Legends and Traditions,* Sikes, 1880.
[89] *Folklore of Wales,* Ross, 2001.

CHAPTER 10

MALEVOLENT CAILLEACH

Some of the tales of the Cailleach have her cast in the role of malevolent hag and spinner of evil spells. This was usually the result of Church propaganda, as may be seen by the way she is compared unfavourably to the Christian figures in the stories. One element that remained true in the stories however is the emphasis on her age which is usually found even in the most negative portrayals.

Looking at the negative portrayals, you can see where positive qualities have been demonized and she has become twisted into a malevolent or hideous figure of fear, a far cry from the benevolent land-shaping lady of the beasts, or priestess guarding the waters and the animals. The mindset which produced the witch trials emphasised a negative view of solitary old women, and so a Cailleach priestess cult if one existed would have been an obvious target for abuse.

1. The Gyre Carling

When we recall the equation of the terms Cailleach and Carlin in Scotland, it is easy to see why the Gyre Carling or Gay Carline (*Old Witch*), should have been described by Sir Walter Scott as the *'mother witch of the Scottish peasantry'*. In private correspondence Scott illustrated her penchant for human flesh by quoting from a poem in the Bannatyne MSS (1568) describing her alleged unpleasant tastes:

> "*Thair dwelt ane grit Gyre Carling in awld Betokis bour, That levit [lived] upoun menis flesche [men's flesh].*"

Gyre Carling carried an iron club (*ane yren club*), which is reminiscent of the rod of winter carried by the Cailleach Bheur. She could also shape-shift, as demonstrated when she was attacked by dogs and shape-shifted into a pig.

> "*The Carling schup [shaped] her on ane sow and is her gaitis [road] gane, Grunting our [over] the Greik sie [Greek Sea].*"[90]

Additionally the Gyre Carling has the power of prophecy, as seen with the Cailleach:

> "*For my guddame, the gyre carling,
> Leird me this prophecy of Marling*"[91]

The Bannatyne Manuscript is not the first reference to the Gyre Carling, as she was mentioned some twenty

---

[90] MSS Bannatyne.
[91] MSS Bannatyne.

years earlier by Dr Leyden in his work *The Complaynt of Scotland* (1549) as the Queen of the Fairies, and subsequently in various works as an interchangeable term with Nicneven and Cailleach.

That she was being belittled and subject to the negative propaganda of the Christian church is made clear through the associations made. For as well as being Queen of the Witches, she was also married to Mohammed and was Queen of the Jews. As Islam and Judaism were two of the chief enemies of the medieval church, it made sense to lump them in with witchcraft as an early complex of spiritual enemies.

> *"The carling now for difpyte*
> *Is mareit [married] with Mahomyte [Mohammed],*
> *And will the doggis interdyte.*
> *For she is quene of Jowis [Jews]."*[92]

2. The Cailleach of Gleann na mBiorach and the Black Bull

A long time ago a Cailleach lived in Gleann na mBiorach in County Kerry, in a cave under a huge rock on the side of the valley. Nobody ever saw her outside of the entrance of the cave, and none of the locals would go past the cave at night, when a huge barking was always heard from inside. It was said that if you went past the cave at night you were never seen again, dragged into the cave to be eaten.[93]

One day an old man called Murchadh Ruadh Ó Conchubhair was carrying a sheaf of oats to feed his black bull which he had pastured grazing in the valley. It

---

92 MSS Bannatyne.
93 Recorded in *An Sgeulaidhe Gaedhealach*, De hÍde, 1933.

was just before sunrise and as the brave old man passed by the Cailleach's cave he saw a heron flying overhead, which dropped a large eel in the cave mouth. As soon as the eel hit the ground an eight-legged white dog came running out of the cave and carried the eel into the cave in its mouth. Murchadh was terrified by this supernatural phenomenon, and commented to the world in general that the Cailleach was indeed an enchanted hag as everybody said.

On hearing this observation the black bull spoke to Murchadh, telling him that the Cailleach had dwelt in the cave there since the time of the Fir Bolgs. She had created a plague which had killed all the cattle in Ireland except the black bull and one cow who was his mate, and as a result he was her deadly enemy. The black bull went on to tell Murchadh that the heron was the Cailleach's mother and the eight-legged dog was her son, and there was only one way to defeat her. He had to gather a large quantity of the bull's droppings and make a fire at the cave entrance. He also had to bring a flail and use it to protect himself from the heron or dog if they attacked him, but not to attack the Cailleach, who the black bull himself would fight.

Murchadh agreed to this plan, but asked the black bull whether he should tell other people that the bull could speak. The bull replied indifferently that he didn't care who Murchadh told, for when he had killed the Cailleach and her family he too would die as he would have achieved his purpose in life.

Murchadh went home and the next morning asked his wife to go and borrow a flail for him to use. His puzzled wife demanded to know why Murchadh should want a flail, as they did not have any oats or wheat to thresh. He would not tell his wife why he wanted the flail, and after finishing his breakfast went and gathered a large quantity of the bull's droppings as he had been instructed and left them on a rock to dry. When he returned home his wife presented him with a flail she had borrowed on his behalf.

The next day, taking his courage in his hands, he went to the cave mouth and made a fire of the dried bull droppings. Soon the flames were jumping high and filling the cave with smoke. Amidst barking and coughing the Cailleach and the white dog came charging out of the cave to escape the overpowering smoke. As they burst forth the black bull charged the white dog. The Cailleach called out a warning to her son, shrieking that he should get a grip on the bull's nose as he was Domblas Mór, her great enemy since the time of the great cattle plague.

The dog leapt at the bull trying to grab his nose, but the black bull was too fast, and tossed him in the air with his horns. As the dog fell Murchadh struck him with the flail splitting his skull. However the white dog was still alive and tried to attack the bull a second time. Again the bull tossed the dog in the air, even higher this time. Murchadh went to strike the dog a second time with the flail but missed as he was attacked by the heron. The heron tried to stab him in the eye but missed and caught him in the middle of the forehead, causing blood to gush everywhere. As he was blinded by the blood, the Cailleach rushed over and started throttling Murchadh until he thought he would die. The black bull saved Murchadh by kicking the hag so hard that she was thrown across the valley.

The Cailleach returned to the fray and insisted the fight be between Murchadh and herself. Ignoring the bull's previous advice, Murchadh agreed but said he needed to redress the balance from the blow he took from her mother, and struck the Cailleach on the forehead with his flail. The Cailleach screamed so loudly it was heard seven miles away, and at this the dog rose up and grabbed Murchadh by the throat.

The black bull ran into action and kicked the dog away, treading him into little pieces. At this the Cailleach cursed them and fell down dead, and the heron tried to attack him again, but Murchadh hit her with the flail and broke her neck, killing her too. The bull congratulated him and told him to go into the cave and take as much gold and silver as he could carry from her hoard.

The bull advised Murchadh to tell people the money was from selling him for a high price, as nobody would ever see him again. Then he encouraged Murchadh to leave quickly, and as he left the cave earth and stones fell blocking the cave entrance forever and leaving the bull inside to die. Murchadh went home and told his wife that he had sold the bull and they lived a happy life on the wealth he had gathered.

3. The Cailleach Bhéarthach and Donnchadh Mór Mac Mánais

Once upon a time a Cailleach and her daughter settled in Glenmaddy. She was extremely wealthy and bought a big house and an estate with horses, cows and sheep to farm. The Cailleach was famous for her thrifty nature, and would only employ labourers who would contract for a six month period, and only pay them at the end of the six months. They had to keep up with her in every type of work and would be fed oatmeal bread and porridge. Of course as she was a magician nobody could keep up with her, though many a young man died trying to work as hard as her. [94]

Now one day Donnchadh Mór Mac Mánais heard the story of how no man could keep up with the Cailleach at work, and decided to prove himself better. He declared that if he could not defeat her he would drown himself. Donnchadh was no ordinary man, for he was as strong as a stallion and fast as a deer.

The next day Donnchadh went to the Cailleach and offered her his services. The Cailleach told him her terms, which were sixty florin pieces, with the same at harvest time and a fat sheep at La Samhna (1st November) if he could toss her over the twenty foot high wall of the field. But if he could not keep up with her on any type of work he would receive no pay. Donnchadh said the sheep sounded like a joke, but if she increased the number of sheep to hurl to a score he would take on as her labourer. The Cailleach agreed, unable to believe any man could perform such a feat.

The next day Donnchadh turned up for work, and as he ate his porridge he noticed the Cailleach's daughter as she sat opposite him at the table. Never had he seen such an ugly girl, but Donnchadh praised her beauty and complimented her, telling her how lovely she was. A day of hard labour such as he had never experienced followed, and by the end of the day Donnchadh had managed to keep up, although the effort had nearly killed him.

---

[94] Recorded in *An Sgeulaidhe Gaedhealach*, De hIde, 1933.

At the end of the day he thought of going home, but knew this would mean he had lost the contest. So instead he cunningly told the Cailleach's daughter that he was in love with her, but the labour would kill him. The daughter replied she also loved him, and could help him so he would not have to do any more hard labour and would become incredibly strong. The daughter knew the Cailleach's secret. She had a magical black hound, and whoever drank the hound's milk would become as strong as sixty men. Every morning she soaked Donnchadh's bread in the milk. Over the next few days Donnchadh went from keeping up to leaving the Cailleach behind when it came to work, to her fury. Frustrated, the Cailleach went to a magician blacksmith she knew and asked him to make her a new magical spade to use to outwit Donnchadh, but this did not help her.

Another time Donnchadh moved in front of the Cailleach, angering her and they fought. The Cailleach swore that no man would ever leave her behind, and he threw her spade away. The Cailleach throttled him, and would surely have killed him had not her daughter interfered and split the pair of them up. After this they worked together peaceably until it was time for mowing the hay.

Now when it came to the hay mowing, the daughter promised to put spikes down to blunt the Cailleach's magical scythe, otherwise Donnchadh would never keep up with her and he would die. As they scythed throw the hay, the Cailleach was puzzled at how tough it was on her scythe, but there was nothing she could do about it.

Once again Donnchadh finished first thanks to the aid of the Cailleach's daughter.

The next task was the reaping of the corn, and again the daughter revealed her mother's secret. A magical beetle dwelt in the handle of her sickle, and as long as it was there she could not be matched at reaping. When they started reaping, the Cailleach forged ahead and taunted Donnchadh. He pretended not to hear properly and rushed to her, knocking the sickle out of her hand and then pulling the handle out and killing the beetle. At this the Cailleach gave him his liberty to leave the next day and his pay if he would keep her secret.

Donnchadh agreed with the Cailleach and she told him her story, revealing it for the first time. She was in fact over one hundred and eighty years old and had been jilted by her lover as a pregnant young girl. So she went to a blacksmith magician and asked for his help gaining magical powers. He agreed and following his directions she ended up gaining the black hound, whose milk she drank, and the beetle he had killed. She killed her ex-lover and his wife, and returned to the smith magician, where her daughter was born. He transformed her appearance so nobody would recognize her, and she worked for forty years on his bellows.

One day she accidentally struck the magician on the thumb with a sledgehammer, and he transformed her into a sow for one hundred years in punishment. At the end of this the magician gave her a bag of gold and silver and reunited her with her daughter and hound and beetle, who had not aged at all in the century past. So the Cailleach travelled to Glenmaddy with her daughter and hound and beetle and settled there.

Donnchadh kept his promise to keep her secret, and when Samhain came he threw the score of sheep over the wall. Soon afterwards the Cailleach got sick, and all the local women came to see if they could help her. However her sickness worsened, and then her house was struck by thunder and lightning, killing her, her daughter and hound. The next day hundreds of hounds surrounded the house, and it was ever after known as Glenmaddy.

4. The Cailleach Mhore of Cilbrick

The Cailleach Mhore was a very rich and wicked old woman, who would never give anything away or ask anyone to sit down in her house. She made the life of anyone who came near her a misery.[95]

Hearing of her ways, a bold man called William laid a wager that he could make her go against her ways. The locals laughed, so William determined to prove himself. He walked into the Cailleach's kitchen, and she demanded to know where he was coming from and where he was going. William replied that he came from the south and was going to the north. Next she asked his name, and he replied his name was William Dean Suidhe. William Dean Suidhe (*sit down*) she repeated, and William bowed and jumped into a seat.

Angered by the presumption of the man, but unable to take her words back, the Cailleach took out a huge round bannock cake shaped like the moon and started eating it. William commented that her piece of cake was very dry, and she replied that the fat side was to her, showing her side which had an inch of butter on it.

---

[95] *Popular Tales of the West Highlands*, Campbell, 1860.

William retorted *"the side that is to you shall be to me"* and grabbed a piece of the cake. Calling her a *"satanic Cailleach"* he ran from her hut with his trophy. She cursed him that he might die from eating the cake, but William wisely did not eat his piece. She however did, and the curse rebounded on her and killed her.

The wealth of the Cailleach in this story hints at her earlier roots as an Earth goddess, as does the motif of the thick layer of butter (see the tale of the *Cailleach Bhéarthach and the Walker* earlier). The comment of the cake being shaped like the moon also hints at an earlier symbolism in the story. However it has been changed into a selfish hag whose magic rebounds on her, a complete denigration of the wisdom of the Cailleach as either Earth goddess or priestess.

5. The Heron of Lock a-na-Cailleach

Amongst the locals around Loch A-na-Cailliach the story was told of the Cailleach who lived in the woods, spreading sickness and death amongst men and beasts.[96] The only person immune to her magic was the local minister, who used to annoy her with his prayers, which pricked her like a pin. Finally the locals appealed to the minister, and he drove her out with holy water. The locals were greatly relieved, until they found out that she had taken up residence at the cairn of stones by the nearby Loch.

The Cailleach was often seen at night, flying as a heron by the moonlight. Despite their best efforts, none of the locals could harm her when they shot at her with

---

[96] *Short Sketches of the Wild Sports and Natural History of the Highlands*, St John, 1846.

their guns. Eventually an old sergeant from one of the highland regiments who was known as a scoundrel loaded his gun with silver buttons and a crooked sixpence instead of normal shot and watched the cairn until she left.

Then he secreted himself in the cairn and waited for her return. Through the night he drank all his smuggled whisky, and sat in ambush. Then at dawn in the mist she returned, and he shot her before swooning with fear. He was found later in the day, unconscious, with his gun burst and his collarbone nearly broken, and a huge heron dead on the ground near the cairn. She stopped causing trouble for the locals after this, though the cairn was avoided at night, as her ghost was reputed to haunt it.

CHAPTER 11

POSSIBLE CAILLEACH DERIVATIVES

Around the British Isles we find a number of figures in local folklore which have characteristics and motifs in common with the Cailleach. It is possible some of these may be derived from her myths and legends, or from a common source, and have become influenced by other local factors. Alternatively it may be a synchronistic combination of similarities.

Such figures are found all around Britain, including Black Annis (England and Scotland), the Glaistig (Scotland), the Old Woman of the Mountain (Wales), Mala Lia (Scotland), Muilidheartach (Scotland), Nicneven (Scotland), Gyre Carling (Scotland) and St Bronagh (Ireland). All of these are discussed subsequently apart from Gyre Carling, who was discussed in the previous chapter.

1. Black Annis

Black Annis was a blue-faced hag found in both English and Scottish folklore, but especially English, which leads us to speculate whether she was a survival of the Cailleach in another guise. She was also known as Black Agnes or Cat Anna (which has been suggested is a corruption of the word Cailleach). Black Annis lived in a cave called Black Annis' Bower Close in the Dane Hills, in Leicestershire, which she dug out with her own long iron nails. There was a mighty oak tree in front of the cave, and Black Annis was in the habit of hiding behind this oak and leaping out to catch stray children and lambs and devour them.

One version of the tale has Black Annis being a nocturnal figure, turning to stone if she ventured out in daylight, recalling the stories of the Cailleach Bheur turning into stone for the summer. People in Leicestershire were terrified of Black Annis, and as most people did not have window-glass until recent centuries, anti-witch-herbs were tied above the apertures to stop Black Annis reaching inside with her very long arms and grabbing their babies.

Every year on Easter Monday (known as Black Monday in honour of Black Annis, suggesting the survival of a divine propitiation ceremony), the local custom was to hold a mock-hare hunt from her cave to the Mayor of Leicester's house. The bait was actually a dead cat rather than a hare, and it was drenched in aniseed. The cat was probably used to symbolise Annis by her name of Cat Anna, and aniseed was used as an anti-witchcraft herb. By the end of the eighteenth century the hunt gave way to an annual event known as the Dane Hills Fair, although her memory lived on, as this description from 1941 shows:

> "Black Annis lived in the Danehills. She was ever
> so tall and had a blue face and had long white

teeth and she ate people. She only went out when it was dark ... when she ground her teeth people could hear her in time to bolt their doors and keep well away from the window ... When Black Annis howled you could hear her five miles away and then even the poor folk in the huts fastened skins across the window and put witch-herbs above it to keep her away safe."[97]

Like the Cailleach, Black Annis could tell the future when it suited her. Her best known prophecy was made when King Richard III struck his spurs on a stone pillar on a bridge on his way to the battle at Bosworth. Annis predicted, *"It will be his head that will hit that stone when he comes back"*. Sure enough after the battle his naked body was thrown across the saddle of a horse and his head it hit the same stone that his spurs had struck.[98]

The Scottish version of Black Annis was known to dwell on the moors and hillsides of the Scottish Highlands. She was described as a witch-like hideous old hag with blue skin and a single piercing eye (akin to some of the Cailleach Beira descriptions). If she captured human beings she would eat them. Descriptions refer to her sitting on a pile of bones outside her cave, by an oak tree (as with the English version).

Black Annis would carry humans off into her cave, suck them completely dry of blood and eat their flesh. Once this was done she would drape the flayed skins out to dry on the oak's branches, to be made into skirts for her to wear. Local shepherds also blamed any lost sheep on her hunger.

---

[97] *Forgotten Folk Tales of the English Counties*, Tongue, 1970.
[98] *Leicestershire and Rutland*, Mee, 1937.

The best known description of this fascinating figure was written by the poet, John Heyrick Jnr, in the 18th century:-

"Where down the plain the winding pathway falls,
From Glen-field, to Lester's ancient walls;
Nature, or art, with imitative power,
Far in the Glenn has plac'd Black Annis's Bower.
An oak, the pride of all the mossy dell,
Spreads its broad arms above the stony cell;
And many a bush, with hostile thorns arrayed,
Forbids the secret cavern to invade;
Whilst delving vales each way meander round,
And violet banks with redolence abound.
Here, if the uncouth song of former days
Soil not the page with Falsehood's artful lays,
Black Annis held her solitary reign,
The dread and wonder of the neighbouring plain.
The shepherd grieved to view his waning flock,
And traced his firstlings to the gloomy rock.
No vagrant children culled the flow'rets then,
For infant blood oft stained the gory den.
Not Sparta's mount,[99] for infant tears renown'd,
Echo'd more frequently the piteous sound.
Oft the gaunt Maid the frantic Mother curs'd,
Whom Britain's wolf with savage nipple nurs'd;
Whom Lester's sons beheld, aghast the scene,
Nor dared to meet the Monster of the Green.
'Tis said the soul of mortal man recoil'd
To view Black Annis's eye, so fierce and wild;
Vast talons, foul with human flesh, there grew
In place of hands, and her features livid blue,
Glar'd in her visage; whilst her obscene waist
Warm skins of human victims embrac'd.
But Time, than Man more certain, tho' more slow,
At length 'gainst Annis drew his sable bow;
The great decree the pious shepherds bless'd,
And general joy the general fear confess'd.

---

[99] A reference to Mount Taygetus, where children were exposed to the elements to see if they lived or died in ancient Spartan society.

Not without terror they the cave survey,
Where hung the monstrous trophies of her sway:
'Tis said, that in the rock large rooms were found,
Scoop'd with her claws beneath the flinty ground;
In these the swains her hated body threw,
But left the entrance still to future view,
That children's children might the tale rehearse,
And bards record it in their tuneful verse.
But in these listless days, the idle bard
Gives to the wind all themes of cold regard;
Forgive, then, if in rough, unpolished song,
An unskilled swain the dying tale prolong.
And you, ye Fair, whom Nature's scenes delight,
If Annis' Bower your vagrant steps invite,
Ere the bright sun Aurora's car succeed,
Or dewy evening quench the thirsty mead,
Forbear with chilling censures to refuse
Some gen'rous tribute to the rustic muse.
A violet or common daisy throw,
Such gifts such as Maro's lovely nymphs bestow;
Then shall your Bard survive the critic's frown,
And in your smiles enjoy his best renown."[100]

2. Glaistig

The Glaistig (alternatively glaistic, glaisnig, glaislig, glaisric or glaislid) was a fairy being who seems to have a lot in common with the Cailleach, suggesting a common root. Her name may mean either water imp or hag, from *glas* meaning *water* and *stic* meaning *imp* (or *hag*).[101] She was sometimes described as being half-woman and half-goat, frequenting lonely lakes and rivers. The Glaistig also took credit for actions ascribed to the Cailleach Bheur, such as the heap of stones known as the Carn-na-Caillich. A Gaelic rhyme quoted her as saying:

---

[100] *County Folklore Printed Extracts No. 3, Leicestershire & Rutland*, Billson, 1895.
[101] Carmichael in *Carmina Gadelica* volume 2:287.

"Know ye the Cailleach's cairn
On that green hillside yonfer?
It was I that gathered it with a creel,
Every pebble that is in it,
To put a bridge on the Sound of Mull –
And to put it there were easy,
Had not the neck-rope broken,
It were there now beyond doubt."[102]

The attributions to the Glaistig were diverse, perhaps because it was the name of a group of beings rather than a single individual. Glaistigs were variously depicted as being very tall or small, either beautiful or wan and haggard, and able to shape shift into a range of animal forms, which include dogs, foals, mares and sheep. They were also said to enjoy herding sheep and cattle (like the Cailleach Bheur).

It was believed that if offerings of milk were left out for them they would herd and look after cattle for people, in the manner of brownies and other helpful fairy creatures. They were also said to look after lonely elderly people and people of simple mind, as well as enjoying playing games with children. At times they would visit houses and ask to come in and dry themselves by the fire, as they would always be dripping wet.

Glaistigs were said to live either in caves, or by water at fords or in a waterfall. They were thought to wail to foretell deaths in old families, in a manner similar to the Banshee. There were also malicious Glaistigs, who would attack travellers at fords. They would question the traveller first, and any weapon or item named by the traveller could not subsequently be used to harm the

---

[102] Translation given in *Scottish Folk-Lore and Folk Life*, MacKenzie, 1935.

Glaistig. A cunning traveller would thus only describe weapons and never name them. These Glaistigs were considered to be members of the Fuath, the class of Scottish faeries associated with water and considered to be particularly dangerous to humans.

3. Juan White

The Old Woman of the Mountain in Wales sounds like a definite Cailleach derivative, being an old woman and associated with mountains. However she is a negative manifestation, having a tendency to lead people astray on the mountains at night or on misty days. Rev. Edmund Jones gave a detailed description of her in his curious work *A Relation of Apparitions of Spirits in the County of Monmouth and the Principality of Wales* (1767):

> *"The Apparition was the resemblance of a poor old woman, with an oblong four-cornered hat, ash-coloured clothes, her apron thrown a-cross her shoulder, with a pot or wooden Can in her hand, such as poor people carry to fetch milk with, always going before them, sometimes crying out wow up. Who ever saw this Apparition, whether by night or in a misty day, though well acquainted with the road, they would be sure to lose their way; for the road appeared quite different to what it really was; and so far sometimes the fascination was, that they thought they were going to their journey's end when they were really going the contrary way. Sometimes they heard her cry wow up, when they did not see her."*

The apron and milk pot are both Cailleach motifs as well, further reinforcing the possible connection, as was the claim that she was a witch. Her name being White also hints at the Cailleach and her wintery powers. However the folklore of the area tells us that the apparitions only began after the death of Juan White. Her range was all across the Black Mountains, with many sightings on the border with Herefordshire on Hatterall Hill.

Sikes mentioned her in his late nineteenth century work *British Goblins: Welsh Folklore, Fairy Mythology, Legends and Traditions* (1880), though by 1912 she was largely forgotten in Herefordshire. Some sources (like Briggs)[103] described her as being one of the Gwyllion, or Welsh fairies, rather than a human.

The folklorist Leather found no reference to her in the early twentieth century except the placing of a bowl of water at the foot of the maypole to keep the Old Woman of the Mountain away at the Mayday festivities at Crasswall near Hay-on-Wye.[104] The timing is significant as Beltane is the traditional time when the Cailleach's rule ends. The water motif is also interesting, though it is an inversion of the usual positive water connections of the Cailleach, being more reminiscent of the old Jewish practice of using bowls of water to contain demons.

4. Mala Lia

Mala Lia (or Liath) means *Grey Eyebrows*, and was the name of a Cailleach who protected swine. She had her own herd which was ruled by a deadly venomous boar, whose bristles would kill anyone they touched. According to some tales Mala Lia was also a cannibal like the Gyre Carling and Black Annis:

---

[103] *The Fairies in Tradition and Literature,* Briggs, 1967.
[104] *Folklore of Herefordshire*, Leather, 1912.

"His lair on Meall-an-Tuirc's rough side
Where Mala Lia' kept her swine –
Witch Mala Lia', evil-eyed,
Foul, shapeless and malign –
Was all begrimed with filth and gore
And horrid with the limbs of men
The unclean monster killed and tore
To feast on in her den."[105]

One day the hero Diarmaid decided to hunt the deadly boar, despite having just eloped with his beautiful wife Grainne. Many a hunter had tried in vain to catch and kill the venomous boar, but nobody ever succeeded. As Diarmaid followed the boar's tracks he passed a raven, pecking at a hare's corpse. The raven spoke to him and told him to turn back or he would die. The headstrong hero ignored the raven and carried on tracking the boar. He passed a boulder topped by a crow, which also told him he would die if he continued his hunt.

Diarmaid ignored the crow as well, and began to close in on the boar. He sneaked towards the boar's lair, only to be taunted by Mala Lia, who appeared and followed him, predicting his death if he attacked the boar. Diarmaid was enraged by her prediction, so he grabbed Mala Lia and threw her over a cliff. He hurried to the boar's lair, and found the venomous boar. Diarmaid then managed to slay the boar, but as it died one of its venomous bristles pierced the inside of his heel, and within minutes Diarmaid too lay dead beside the boar. Mala Lia returned to find the corpses at the lair, both far more mortal than she was.

---

[105] *The Venomous Wild Boar of Glen Glass*, Sutherland, 1892

5. Muilidheartach

> *"There were two slender spears of battle upon either side of the hag; her face was blue-black, the lustre of coal and her bone tufted tooth was like rusted bone. In her head was one deep pool-like eye swifter than a star in a winter sky; upon her head gnarled brushwood like the clawed old wood of aspen root."*[106]

The Muilidheartach[107] was described as a watery form of the Scottish Cailleach Bheur. When in the water she was described as being reptilian. However she could also assume the form of a hag, with the ability to raise winds and sea-storms.

The Muilidheartach was considered a dangerous water fairy, being one of the Fuath class of fairies, characterized by a tendency to appear as a hag at the door, dripping wet and begging to be allowed to dry herself by the fire. A refusal would result in her growing in size and ferocity, with behaviour that made the unfortunate person regret their refusal.[108]

6. Nicneven

Scott mentioned the alternative name of Nicneven for the Gyre Carling in *Minstrelsy of the Scottish Border* (1821). Nicneven was also described in other works from this period as *"the Hecate of Scottish necromancy"*. She first appeared in literature in *The Flyting of Dunbar and Kennedy* (1508) as a giant malignant hag, establishing her connection with the Cailleach as another expression

---

[106] *Popular Tales of the West Highlands*, Campbell, 1860
[107] Pronounced *"moolyarstuch"*.
[108] *Scottish Folk-Lore and Folk Life*, MacKenzie, 1935.

of the same type of spiritual creature. Later in the sixteenth century she was again seen in *The Flyting of Montgomery and Polwart* (1585) where it said of her:

"*Nicneven and her nymphs, in numbers anew, With charms from Caitness, and Chanrie in Ross.*"

The name Nicneven has been suggested as meaning '*destroying or demonical Neptune*',[109] which certainly maintains the watery connection of a figure who commands nymphs. However it is more likely that it refers to the connection between the Cailleach and Ben Nevis, her mountain home. Nic means *daughter of* and Neven is derived from Nevis, so in fact Nicneven means Daughter of Nevis, a suitable appellation for the Cailleach.

In *A Etymological Dictionary of the Scottish Language* (1825), Nicneven is mentioned as the Queen of the Fairies, referring to a quote about Gyre Carling by Leyden from his sixteenth century work *The Complaynt of Scotland* (1549).

It is also interesting to note that Scott used the name to describe the head of a coven of witches, as seen in his *Letters on Demonology and Witchcraft* (1830) where he wrote, "*After midnight the sorceress Marion MacIngarach, the chief priestess or Nicneven of the company*" when describing the necromantic activities of a coven. By this point the term was being used interchangeably with Gyre Carling for a senior witch. On this point we may recall Mackay's comment that "*witches are only fossil*

---

[109] *Illustrations of Shakespeare, and of Ancient Manners*, Douce, 1839.

priestesses,"[110] and return to speculation about the survival of a priestess cult in degenerated form.

7. St Bronagh

The name Bronagh comes from the same root as Bronach, a name sometimes applied to the Cailleach Béarra in Ireland. Bronach appears in the local Irish folklore of the Cliffs of Moher, which have at their southern point a rock formation known as the Hag's Head due to its resemblance to a woman's head looking out to sea.

Bronagh means *sad* or *sorrowful,* which fits with stories like the *Lament of the Old Woman of Beara.* St Bronagh was a sixth century woman who became an Abbess after having a vision and setting up a monastic community. She adopted Christianity from St Patrick when he returned to Ireland. Her feast day is the 2nd April.

Considering the stories where St Patrick makes the Cailleach disappear in a red flash, demonstrating his *superiority,* this strongly suggests a case of assimilation of the old goddess, as the church did for many other Celtic deities.

---

[110] *The Deer-Cult & the Deer-Goddess Gult of the Ancient Caledonians,* Mackay, 1932.

BIBLIOGRAPHY

Ainsworth, William Harrison; *Ainsworth's Magazine: A Miscellany of Romance, General Literature, and Art* Vol XV; 1849; Chapman & Hall; London

Billington, Sandra & Green, Miranda (eds); *The Concept of the Goddess*; 1996; Routledge; London

Billson, C.J.; *County Folklore Printed Extracts No. 3, Leicestershire & Rutland*; 1895.

Borlase, William Copeland; *The Dolmens of Ireland, Their Distribution, Structural Characteristics, and Affinities in Other Countries*; 1897; Chapman & Hall; London

Branston, Brian; *The Lost Gods of England*; 1974; Oxford University Press; Oxford

Briggs, K.M.; *The Fairies in Tradition and Literature*; 1967; Routledge & Kegan Paul; London

Campbell, J.F.; *Popular Tales of the West Highlands*; 1860; Alexander Gardner; London

Campbell, J.G.; *Superstitions of the Highlands & Islands of Scotland*; 1900; James MacLehose; Glasgow

----------; *Witchcraft and Second Sight in the Highlands and Islands of Scotland*; 1902; James MacLehose; Glasgow

Carey, John; *Transmutations of Immortality in 'The Lament of the Old Woman of Beare'*; 1999; in *Celtica* 23:30-37

----------; *Did the Irish Come from Spain? The Legend of the Milesians*; 2001; in History Ireland Autumn:8-11

Carmichael, Alexander; *Carmina Gadelica*; 1900; Carmichael; Edinburgh

Crualaoich, Gearóid Ó; *The Book of the Cailleach*; 2003; Cork University Press; Cork

----------; *Continuity and Adaptation in Legends of Cailleach Bhéarra*; 1988 in *Bealoideas* 56:153-78

Curtis, M.R. & G.R.; *Callanish: the Stones, and Moon, and the Sacred Landscape*; 1994; Curtis & Curtis; Callanish

Dalton, G.F.; *The Loathly Lady: A Suggested Interpretation*; 1971; in *Folklore* 82:124-31

Dalyell, John Graham; *The Darker Superstitions of Scotland*; 1834; Waugh and Innes; Edinburgh

Daniélou, Alain; *The Myths and Gods of India*; 1991; Inner Traditions International; Vermont

Davidson, H.R.E.; *Myths and Symbols in Pagan Europe: Early Scandinavian and Celtic Religions*; 1988, Manchester University Press; Manchester

-----------; *Roles of the Northern Goddess*; 1998; Routledge; London

-----------; *Weland the Smith*; 1958; in *Folklore* 69:145-59.

Douce, Francis; *Illustrations of Shakespeare, and of Ancient Manners*; 1839; London

Ford, Doug; *The Megalith Builders*; no date; www.jerseyheritagetrust.org/edu/downloads/The%20Megalith %20Builders.doc

Geddes, Arthur; *Scots Gaelic Tales of Herding Deer or Reindeer Traditions of the Habitat and Transhumance of Semi-Domesticated "Deer", and of Race Rivalry*; 1951; in *Folklore* 62:2:296-311

Giles, J.A.; *The Works of Gildas and Nennius Translated from the Latin*; 1841; J Bohn; London

Gill, W. Walter; *A Manx Scrapbook*; 1929; J W Arrowsmith; Bristol

Grant, Katherine Whyte; *Myth, Tradition and Story from Western Argyll*; 1925; Oban Times Press; Oban

Gregory, Lady Augusta; *Gods and Fighting Men: The Story of the Tuatha De Danann and of the Fianna of Ireland*; 1904; J Murray; London

Groome, Francis H.; *Ordnance Gazetteer of Scotland* (6 vols); 1896; William Mackenzie; Edinburgh

Gwynn, Edward (ed, trans); *The Metrical Dindshenchas (Vol 3)*; 1913; Royal Irish Academy; Dublin

Harrison, William (ed); *Mona Miscellany: A Selection of Proverbs, Sayings, Ballads, Customs, Superstitions, and Legends, Peculiar to the Isle of Man*; 1873; Manx Society; Douglas

Hope, A.D.; *A Midsummer Eve's Dream: variations on a theme by William Dunbar*; 1970; Canberra

Hull, Eleanor; *Legends and Traditions of the Cailleach Bheara or Old Woman (Hag) of Beare*; 1927; in *Folklore* 38.3:225-54

Hull, Vernam; *Expulsion of the Dessi*; 1957; in *Zeitschrift für Celtische Philologie* vol. 57

James, E.O.; *Origins of Sacrifice*; 1971; Kennikat Press; New York

Jamieson, John; *A Etymological Dictionary of the Scottish Language*; 1825; W & C Tait; Edinburgh

John, Ewart Simpkins; *Examples of Printed Folk-lore Concerning Fife with Some Notes on Clackmannan and Kinross-shire*; 1914; Folklore Society; London

Jones, Edmund; *A Relation of Apparitions of Spirits in the County of Monmouth and the Principality of Wales*; 1767; Newport

Karlsdottir, Alice; *Magic of the Norse Goddesses*; 2003; Runa-Raven Press; Texas

Keding, Dan, & Douglas, Amy; *English Folktales*; 2005; Libraries Unlimited; Westport

Kelly, Walter Keating; *Curiosities of Indo-European Tradition and Folk-lore*; 1863; Chapman & Hall; London

Kinsella, Thomas (trans); *The Tain*; 1970; Oxford University Press; Oxford

Krappe, Alexander H; *La Cailleach Bhéara: Notes de mythologie gaelique*; in *Etudes Celtiques* 1:292-302

Leather, Ella Mary; *Folk-Lore of Herefordshire*; 1912; Jakeman and Carver; Hereford

Leslie, Forbes; *The Early Races of Scotland and Their Monuments*; 1866; Edmonston & Douglas; Edinburgh

List, Edgar A.; *Is Frau Holda the Virgin Mary?*; 1956 in *German Quarterly* 29.2:80-84

Long, G. (ed); *The Penny Cyclopædia Vol III: Athanaric – Bassano*; 1835; Charles Knight; London

Lotte, Motz; *The Winter Goddess: Percht, Holda and Related Figures*; 1984; in *Folklore* 95:2:151-166

Luján, Eugenio R.: *Ptolemy's 'Callaecia' and the language(s) of the 'Callaeci'*; 1999; in *Ptolemy: towards a linguistic atlas of the earliest Celtic place-names of Europe : papers from a workshop sponsored by the British Academy*; CMCS Publications

MacCulloch, J.; *History of the West Highlands*; 1924; Edinburgh

Mackay, J.G.; *The Deer-Cult and the Deer-Goddess Cult of the Ancient Caledonians*; 1932; in *Folklore* 43.2:144-174

Mackenzie, Donald; *Wonder Tales from Scottish Myth and Legend*; 1917; Blackie & Son Ltd, Glasgow

----------; *Scottish Folk-Lore and Folk Life*; 1935; Blackie & Son; London

-----------; *Myths of Babylonia and Assyria*; 1915; Gresham Publishing Company; London

-----------; *A Highland Goddess*; 1912; in *The Celtic Review* Vol 7 No 28:336-345

Maclagan, Robert Craig; *Religio Scotica: Its Nature as Traceable in Scotic Saintly Tradition*; 1909; Otto Schulze & Company; Edinburgh

Magrath, John Mac Rory; *Caithréimm Thoirdhealbhaigh*; 1929; Simpkin Marshall Limited; London

Markale, Jean; *The Epics of Celtic Ireland: Ancient Tales of Mystery and Magic*; 2000; Inner Traditions; Vermont

McNeill, Florence Marian; *The Silver Bough Vol 1: Scottish Folklore & Folk Belief*; 1957; William Maclellan; Glasgow

Mee, Arthur; *Leicestershire and Rutland*; 1937; Hodder & Stoughton; London

Menefee, Samuel Pyeatt; *Meg and Her Daughters: Some Traces of Goddess Beliefs in Megalithic Folklore?*; 1996; in The Concept of the Goddess; Routledge; London

Miller, Hugh; *Scenes and Legends of the North of Scotland*; 1835; Johnstone & Hunter; London

Murphy, Gerard; *The Lament of the Old Woman of Beare*; 1953 in *Proceedings of the Royal Irish Academy* 55:84-109

Newall, Venetia (ed); *The Witch Figure*; 1973; Routledge; London

Noble, Thomas; *The History and Gazetteer of the County of Derby*; 1831; Stephen Glover; Derby

Paredes, Xoán; *Curiosities across the Atlantic: a brief summary of some of the Irish-Galician classical folkloric similarities nowadays. Galician singularities for the Irish*; 2000; in *Chimera*, Dept. of Geography, University College Cork, Ireland

Parsons, David & Sims-Williams, Patrick (eds); *Ptolemy: towards a linguistic atlas of the earliest Celtic place-names of Europe: papers from a workshop sponsored by the British Academy*; 1999; CMCS Publications

Pennant, Thomas; *A Tour in Scotland and Voyage to the Hebrides, 1772*; 1776; Benjamin White; London

Pennick, Nigel; *Celtic Sacred Landscapes*; 1996; Thames & Hudson; London

Poska, Allyson M.; *Women and Authority in Early Modern Spain: The Peasants of Galicia*; 2005; Oxford University Press; Oxford

Rankine, David & d'Este, Sorita; *The Guises of the Morrigan*; 2005; Avalonia; London

Ross, Anne; *Pagan Celtic Britain*; 1967; Routledge & Kegan Paul; London

----------; *Folklore in Wales*; 2001; Tempus; Stroud

Rowling, Marjorie; *Folklore of the Lake District*; 1976; Batsford; London

Savona-Ventura, C, & Mifsud, A.; *Prehistoric Medicine in Malta*; 1999; Savona-Ventura & Mifsud; Malta

Scott, Walter; *Minstrelsy of the Scottish Border*; 1821; A Constable & Co; Edinburgh

-----------; *Letters on Demonology and Witchcraft*; 1830; John Murray; London

Scrope, William; *The Art of Deer-Stalking*; 1839; John Murray; London

Seton, Gordon; *Highways and Byways in the Central Highlands*; 2007; Read Books; Warwickshire

Sibbald, J.; *Chronicle of Scottish Poetry: from the Thirteenth Century to the Union of the Crowns*; 1802; C. Stewart & Co; Edinburgh

Sikes, Wirt; *British Goblins: Welsh Folklore, Fairy Mythology, Legends and Traditions*; 1880; Sampson Low; London

Smith, A.H.; *The Place-Names of the North Riding of Yorkshire*; 1928; Cambridgeshire University Press; Cambridge

S.M.R.; *Cailleach Beinn Na Bric*; 1823, in *The Emmet* Vol 1:40-41; Purvis & Aitken; Glasgow

Society for the Benefit of the Sons and Daughters of the Clergy; *The New Statistical Account of Scotland*; 1845; W Blackwood & Sons; Edinburgh

Spence, Lewis; *The Minor Traditions of British Mythology*; 1948; Rider; London

St John, C.; *Short Sketches of the Wild Sports and Natural History of the Highlands*; 1846; London

Stokes, Whitley; *The Songs of Buchet's House (Esnada Tige Buchet)*; 1904; in *Revue Celtique* 25:18-38, 225-7.

Strabo; *The Geography of Strabo*; 1949; Harvard University Press; Cambridge

Sutherland, Dr Arthur; *The Venomous Wild Boar of Glen Glass*; 1892; in *The Highland Monthly* 4:491

Thierling, Insa; *More than Winter's Crone: The Cailleach in Scotland*; 2001; Tooth & Claw

Tongue, R.L.; *Forgotten Folk Tales of the English Counties*; 1970; Routledge; London

Various; *Transactions of the Gaelic Society of Inverness;* Volume 26:277-9; 1904

Various: *The Monthly Magazine*; 1808; Vol 26:2; Richard Phillips; London

Wood-Martin, W.G.; *Traces of the Elder Faiths of Ireland*; 1902; Longmans Green & Co; London

Wright, Thomas; *On the Local Legends of Shropshire*; 1843; in *Collecteana Archaeologica* Vol 1:50-66; Longman Green Longman & Roberts; London

Yeats, W.B.; *Fairy and Folk Tales of the Irish Peasantry*; 1888; Walter Scott; London

INDEX

.

Lightning Source UK Ltd.
Milton Keynes UK
UKHW02f1337040718
325219UK00011B/667/P

9 781905 297245